I. was
part the retreat —

For Faith
with love,
Pearl

May 1978

BE SWIFT TO LOVE

BE SWIFT TO LOVE

BY BARBARA HOWARD

Life is short and we have not too much time for gladdening the hearts of those who are traveling the dark way with us. Oh, be swift to love! Make haste to be kind.—Henri Amiel

dedication

This fall, when tree planting time arrived, our family planted a tree given to us by neighbors in memory of my father who died this past summer. We gathered around the tree on which we had tied six helium-filled balloons, read some favorite scriptures, and sang "Amazing Grace" (it was my father's favorite hymn as far back as I can remember). When the tree was planted, each family member released one of the balloons. I believe this ritual has enriched our family's worship life.

Our children did not know my father well. They are conscious that he is part of a past about which they know little but from which they have received much. I have shared stories about our fishing trips, picking figs, trips to Brewton and Dixonville, and the times when age and values separated Dad and me.

While the children have heard these stories, they have also shared experiences in our family which they often recall. We like to sit around the dinner table when we are all together and "remember when." Some of our stories are funny, others serious, but they hold special meaning to us because they are part of who we are as persons.

Worship is a shared story. It is our story and His story. Worship is sharing the action of God in our lives. My early family, so different from that of my own children and husband, are part of my story. I celebrate that past—with its pain and joy and ambiguity—and the family which gave it meaning. And I give thanks to my family today—the children from whom I have learned so much and Dick with whom creating our history has been a process of joy and becoming.

contents

fOREWORÒ

Worship is the attitude and action which recognizes the values inherent in and to be received from the object of our worship. When we worship God we are awed by the ultimate values of love and intelligence and understanding which are expressed in his power and purpose. We do not fully sense these values because of our own limitations, but we hope to share in them through our communion with Him in whom we believe they are infinite qualities.

We learn the relationships and values of our humanity by participating in the lives of other human beings. Shall we not also learn the relationships and values of Deity by participating in the life of the Holy Spirit? Such participation goes far beyond our deliberate acts of worship. It also exceeds our spontaneous responses to truth and beauty. When our worship is deliberate and intentional, however, we find ourselves participating emotionally, physically, and intellectually in acts which raise the level of our awareness of the Divine Presence. Becoming more godly thus includes growing consciousness of our participation in the love and intelligence and actions of God.

Reference by the author to Amiel's exhortation to "be swift to love" is itself an act of worship, for God is love. To know this through adoration is to become more loving. This is the purpose of worship—to share in the qualities of the Adored One. He is of ultimate worth. Our response is to recognize his "worth-ship."

Suggestions in this book are particularly suited to family worship. It is most appropriate that in the same primary relationships in which we learn the forms and values of our humanity we should also participate in experiences in which we grow in godliness.

Maurice L. Draper
The First Presidency

an introduction

The material in this book is intended to stimulate and encourage families in their exploration of meaningful ways to participate in worship. The readings need not be used as they are written. They are intended to sensitize persons to the possibilities for worship that are ever present. Ideally, each family will design activities unique to the setting in which the family experiences life together.

In families with small children you may wish to use simpler versions of the Scripture. Paraphrasing in language familiar to the child may be even more effective.

It is important to recognize that many activities in this book may not fit the needs of your family. The most valuable contribution the book can make is to stimulate families to develop their *own* expressions of worship. Spontaneity is one of the facets of creativity which is most often overlooked. Being sensitive to the needs of one another and the community, being aware of ways to express gratitude and praise to God in a way which truly represents the members of your family is indicative of a family engaged in worship.

Evaluate your experiences together. Encourage an honest, critical view of what is happening. Be certain that each person hears every other person. Stay flexible. If you plan to use a suggested outline and at the last moment it seems inappropriate, dismiss the outline and move with the spirit of the family. Persons are more important than any printed material.

Material is provided in a wide age range. In some activities voices are listed as Voice 1 through Voice 6. This can be changed according to the size of your family. It is not necessary for parents to conduct the services on behalf of the children. In most of the activities any member of the family with relatively good reading skills can use the resource and develop the worship. Frequently family members are spoken of as he/she; this is a reminder of the infinite worth of both male and female.

A list of resources will be found in the back of the book. If they are referred to specifically, this will be noted. Some of these resources can be helpful in continuing the search for effective ways to worship as a family in community.

On some occasions, the word "liturgy" is used. This is not to suggest that the family engage in some ritual foreign to the background and beliefs of its members. Rather, "liturgy" may be used here in the meaning of its root words: "the work of the people." What your family develops as an expression of praise, thanksgiving, and commitment to God is indeed the liturgy of your family. Hopefully, new ways will open up to you, and your life together can become this expression.

WORSHIP
ITS MEANINGS

Evelyn Underhill affirms that "worship is the response of the creature to the eternal. . . . Thus worship may be overt or direct, unconscious or conscious. . . . Worship is an acknowledgement of transcendence . . . of a Reality independent of the worshiper, which is always more or less deeply colored by mystery, and which is there first."

Worship, then, is an experience involving the imagination, feelings, and reasoning mind of the participant. Throughout history worship has

embodied images, symbols, rituals—expressions of a yearning for meaning in life.

In a family the understanding of worship will set the tone of what is done as worship. There may be several principles which will enrich your family's appreciation of the experience. Perhaps through the year as you worship together you may develop an awareness of the expression of these principles.

We are tied to the roots of our past—our history is accepted in worship. At the same time we are set free through worship to live in the present moment. There are paradoxes which express this. Worship is continuous and discontinuous. We are related to our past, our record as a family. Yet we are continually living in a condition of change. Not only are children growing into independence but roles and images of each person in the family are in a state of flux. We are culture bound as families at the same time we are culture enriched.

Our worship is local as well as international. Our family circle is unique, yet part of the common family of humanity. We cannot simply pray that trite prayer, "Bless me and my wife, my son John and his wife. Us four, no more. Amen." No Christian family can remain unaffected by the suffering and hunger of other persons. We need to be aware of the rich offerings other cultures provide. There is treasure in the diversity of the world of today. Humanity should be at the heart of our prayers.

Our worship in the family is both denominational and ecumenical. We often sing hymns, read stories, and observe traditions that are rooted in a history larger than our own denomination. In homes where

14

the parents share different backgrounds of faith, the worship life can be a strengthening aspect of the relationship of the family. A deep appreciation for the heritage of each person can bring a sense of community in the home.

Our worship is both religious and secular. The reminder of God acting in our world may greet us with the morning paper. We may find this same living, present God in the records of the Scripture. To use one does not deny the value of the other. Families need both expressions of God's word to sustain them. Children particularly need to see God at work in the sad and lonely places of life as well as in the joyful, happy moments. A ten-year-old boy recently ended the day with the prayer, "Thank you for the good and bad things that have happened to me today." Not sure he had heard right, the father asked his son what he had said. The boy replied, "I thanked God for the good and bad things that happened to me today, Dad. You see, that's my life—and I'm grateful for all my life." To affirm God's presence even when he seems absent from us is indeed to affirm his presence.

The Psalms enrich our understanding of this principle: "The whole world is mine and the fullness thereof." The integrative quality of life is stressed in the Doctrine and Covenants: "All things are both spiritual and temporal." The purpose of the family is to equip persons to live in a world in which responsible choices must be made. The family is not a refuge from the cares of the world. It may be seen as a laboratory for living or a center for reconciliation. But our family life experiences should enable us to be more sensitive to the Christ who appears to us in the hungry, the thirsty,

15

the naked, the sick or imprisoned as described in Matthew 25. Perhaps the genuine measure of the quality of worship can be found in the degree of concern the family shows for those outside its circle.

Members of the family who meet in worship will discover that they sense not only a personal source of strength but also a great social responsibility. We are participating in a gospel of good news. To find only comfort and personal encouragement would scarcely be worship. Mission becomes the way the family lives out its understanding of God's concern for them individually as well as corporately. Paul Waitman Hoon reminds us that "worship is always to be shot through and through with the claim to love and to serve." The worship in which we engage points us to persons who have needs which we can meet. The true meaning of Christian worship is found in the Philippian letter in which the apostle Paul bears witness of the reality of the action of God to human beings in Jesus Christ: "God was in Christ, reconciling the world unto himself, not imputing their trespasses unto them; and hath committed unto us the word of reconciliation."

This witness of grace is the criterion of genuine worship. However, the Holy Spirit cannot be manipulated or controlled. There may be times in your life as a family when, without preparation or plan, you experience what is to you an authentic expression of worship. There may be other times when with the greatest degree of concern you plan a time for the family to gather in worship and the experience has little meaning. This is not to suggest that planning is unnecessary. It does mean that there ought to be spontaneity in worship. It also is confirmation that the Holy Spirit is not under human control.

There are some elements in worship which will be helpful to remember even in spontaneous moments. Worship is not simply a good feeling. Worship is confronting the deepest reality of life as well as ourselves. Worship will contain praise or gratitude. Persons will become aware of their separation from God and each other and will be able to confess their brokenness. But as the scripture has stated, we have been given the word of reconciliation. God has forgiven our sins in Jesus. We are free from the burden of sin.

In worship we are confronted by the Word of God. This is more than the record of the Scriptures. The Word denotes the presence of God in his word, his action and creation. Geoffrey Spencer states:

We usually acknowledge that word and deed are not separate things in a person's relation to us: a man is as good as his word. The central idea is that a word *communicates.* It is the means by which one person makes himself known to another, and reveals his nature. A person communicates at least as much by what he does as by the noises that come from his mouth. So the biblical and more comprehensive view of "word" suggests that the word of God refers to God's communication with us through his participation in our experience.

This word should be part of our worship. To have confronted the demands of the word of God is to have received the commission to "Go . . . be . . . do." There is a sense in which the offering of ourselves is the final act of all worship. This is best expressed in Romans 12, Paul's moving statement on faith. Families that worship are sent as God's offering to his world.

The purpose of worship in the home is not to teach a set of doctrinal principles, though certainly some of this will occur. It is not to memorize the Scriptures, though by their use new understandings should emerge. It is not even to help families understand each other more effectively, though this may grow out of the corporate experience. The purpose of all worship is to confront the Word which is to be understood in its full meaning as the self-disclosure or revelation of God. The sense of reality of his presence and participation in our lives is the witness of our worship as families.

WORShip

the CENtER of LiFE in the family

"Worship is at the very center of life, giving meaning to all that we do."
—James White in *New Forms of Worship.*

One of the problems of families is that worship is planned sometimes as a guilt response to the cry, "We need to get back to the family altar" or "The family that prays together stays together" or some other statement which reminds parents that much time has passed since the family met in worship. For the family to worship corporately there must be a consenting agreement on the part of those who gather that worship will be a meaningful activity.

Before planning specific activities you will need to call all members of your family together and discuss their attitudes toward the nature and purpose of worship. Following this discussion you may want to decide if, as a family, you need to establish specific times for worship. "I hate to sit while Dad preaches to us," one young man said in a Zion's League class at reunion. "You think that's bad?" another asked. "What if your family was reading a chapter of Scripture aloud every morning at breakfast? I just about threw up when we got to the flies and gnats and river of blood and dead fish in the story of Moses!"

Parents would do well to hear the needs of the children (who, in turn, should consider the concerns of their parents). Ross Snyder says, "A family is a group of people who actively approve of each other. . . . A prevailing atmosphere of blaming . . . is not really family *climate*. A family . . . doesn't try to produce character through harping on a member's short-comings and failures.

"A family is a center of healing. . . . A family is a mutuality which personalizes its members. . . . To participate in a family is to enlist in the quiet, persistent out-wearying of hatred by love." Snyder goes on to describe the family as a place where in the midst of tension persons work to help each member feel accepted and whole. He suggests that this is not easy and that there are many pressures outside the family as well as within which make living together in love difficult. But he asserts that this is possible when members of a family are looking together in the same direction—toward God. For love and creativeness come not from merely looking at each other but from looking together toward a greater-than-any-of-us.

Therefore, at the heart of our creative family life is an awareness of the power beyond human definition which enables us not only to be ourselves but to be in relationship to one another. This does not just happen, however. As a family we need to be intentional about the use of time or a genuine worship life may never occur. We do not slap a scripture and prayer on a group of people and label this "worship." Nor can we sandwich between the recreation of a Tuesday night movie on television and the regular evening phone calls a five-minute "worship break." The movie may be an instrument in the activity of worship. But this is most likely to happen through planning.

I believe that church organizations can be detrimental to families sharing in meaningful worship in the setting of the home unless members of the family are equally intentional about how much time is spent in meetings. The family needs to determine together the best time to share. Each family is a unique structure. Some couples with very young children have an evening ritual of story, song, and prayer time which has great meaning in the lives of the children. This may serve as a time for worship in this period in the life of the family. However, the parents may want to introduce into the nightly gathering some new symbols which will enable even a young child to sense something of the wonder of God's love and the meaning of sharing that love. An excellent resource for this is found in a series of little books published by Paulist Press entitled *Rejoice*. The set costs $2.00 and introduces concepts about worship which can be used by parents to enhance family life and to create an awareness in children of the "greater-than-any-of-us." (Please see the Bibliography for other resources.)

Another helpful printed resource for a family is a book by Jack Lundin called *Celebration for Special Days and Occasions*. As a pastor announcing the week's activities at church one Sunday, the author suddenly realized how fragmented the family could become by participation in the endless round of meetings and committees. His book grew out of a need to provide suggestions for special times when the family can worship together. He suggests that the family use a special "cup of blessing," derived from the Hebrew tradition, at these times. Some of the "special times" suggested, with a short liturgy provided, are "When we have been angry and have made up," "On the death of a pet," "When a new child is expected." Lundin also provides liturgies for holidays including Valentine's Day as well as Christmas and Easter.

The family has rich potential for worship life together. It has, usually, a common language, many rich memories, and an intimacy which can create a climate of trust. Henry Horn in *Worship in Crisis* states: "The language of worship . . . demands the use of words which are already filled with meaning by the acts of God and the experience of Christian people." I know two junior high age children who invented words to use to describe anger and love. The family was able to use those words in a special way in a discussion of reconciliation.

Another way the family can develop a life-style of worship is to promote a deeper understanding of the Christian calendar. The Restoration Church has just begun to explore this rich historic tradition. The Christian year had its genesis in the second and third centuries when the believers of Christ began to formalize holidays to observe events in his life. This was an attempt to concretize the action of God in a way that it became part of the story of the believer rather than some abstract principle. When the Jews wanted to express gratitude for God's saving power, they did not speak in theological language about the nature of God. Instead, they told about the marvelous experience of the Passover or the crossing of the Red Sea. The early Christians who wanted to talk about the saving power of God in Jesus told stories which included a manger in Bethlehem or a gathering of men with a cup and bread and wine. They told the story of a painful death and the reality of the resurrection.

The Christian calendar in a limited way has been part of our tradition. We have always celebrated Jesus' birth and his promise of new life at Easter. This is the rhythm of the life of the believer. We come to realize that God cares enough about us to become like us—to identify with our pain and sin. This awareness wakes in us a response and allows us to become new persons. This occurs over and over again, and the festivities throughout the year can symbolize this effectively. Thomas Oden helps us see the meaning of our celebrations:

The Christian year rehearses twice a year in threefold cycles the central themes of Christian existence.

Advent, Christmas, and Epiphany—the first cycle of the Christian year—cluster around the *Incarnation*. Lent, Easter, and Trinity Season—the second cycle of the Christian year—cluster around the Resurrection. Incarnation and Resurrection constitute the two focal events of God's own ministry to the world in Jesus Christ, and they rightly appear therefore, as the two climactic events of the Christian year.

In the Restoration church we might speak of these as the weeks before Christmas, Christmas, and the weeks after, with the same designation for Easter. During these special seasons we recognize that something has happened which has changed the meaning of all life.

We can mark these special times with worship together. We can use advent wreaths, and each Sunday before Christmas Eve for four weeks we can light a new candle, read a scripture, and sing a carol. Although this is an exciting time of year, with secrets and preparations for gift-giving, it is also a time to remember the real purpose of the festivities.

The Christian year can be enhanced by adding to the designated times some important dates that remind the family of God's action in the lives of its members. Birthdays, anniversaries, a new job, graduation into another grade in school, the first baby-sitting job, even some of the sad times like losing a school election or the death of someone in the neighborhood are occasions when the ever present love of God can be celebrated.

The American Bible Society translation of the Psalms in modern English, an inexpensive paperbound volume, can help develop an appreciation for the struggle men have had through the ages to understand the wonder of God and the complexity of human experience.

One family has found that coming together once a week in "family council" has helped develop more opportunities for worship. Sometimes the agenda of the family council is crowded with feelings of rejection and hostility. The purpose of the council is to provide a place where every member of the family may affirm the feelings which are his or hers. No one need defend his actions or attitudes. No one is allowed to criticize another. The purpose of the council is to "claim one's own feelings." Often the members of the family will decide to celebrate the action of God in their history. Scriptures are read, memories are shared, persons respond to statements like "I have seen reconciling love shown today in . . ." or "Today I have cause to celebrate . . ." or "I saw someone who needed help today . . ." or "My goal as a Christian this week is to. . . . " Other times the Scripture reading will relate to some current event. Family members then talk about what the word of God means in their human situation. Sometimes prayers are the major activity of the time together—prayers for the family, the community, the world.

Not every family gathering is worship. There must be present in worship more than just "trying to understand each other." The celebration of the Christian year is more than the remembering of our own joyful experiences. Indeed the Christian year suggests for us all that a decisive life is one filled with suffering on behalf of others. This has running through it the celebrative note. When we remember the death of Jesus and his resurrection we celebrate. When we confront the demands placed on us in our daily lives we celebrate that God has called us to live in this time.

Worship in the family as worship in the congregation is not just a warm feeling of fellowship. Nor is the experience a family may have in the outdoor beauty necessarily worship. It may contain some element of worship, but to call the appreciation of God in nature worship is to reflect a pantheism that is not Christian. Worship calls us to respond to the needs about us. Families who view a polluted stream and feel the pain of the irresponsibility of persons and begin to clean the stream may come closer to the meaning of worship than families who sit around campfires in an outdoor setting and talk about the beautiful creation of God.

Restoration families are called to be God's agents of reconciliation. There is a need to be sustained by the memory of what he has done as it is recorded in Scripture, but the family also needs to be keenly aware of how he is working in the world today. Christian worship promises to transfigure the life of the family. Planning, sharing, celebrating together through the year can provide the family with an enriched understanding of worship.

the christian calendar

The Christian calendar, throughout the centuries, has come to represent the story of our lives under God. There is a rhythm in life. There is a rhythm in worship. The calendar exemplifies the rhythm.

Hopefully some of the seasons of the Christian calendar in our tradition which have not been emphasized may take on new significance as we observe the Christian year. We wait for meaning, we experience meaning, and we give ourselves to this meaning. We are born, we live, we die, and the cycle continues. The calendar reminds us of the events in the life of a Christian: we encounter God, we sense our unworthiness, we experience his acceptance, we accept his claim on us, we respond by moving out under his Spirit to be his people. Advent is a time of anticipation—something is going to happen. Christmas is the story of a happening. Epiphany is what is done about what happened. The same is true of Lent, Easter, and Trinity.

The seasons of Advent and Lent represent the human predicament. Sin, bondage, and the old self represent the condition in which we find ourselves as we yearn for hope and new possibilities. These are seasons of waiting and yearning.

The seasons of Christmas and Easter exemplify God's action in our history. He has come into our experience. He has given himself on our behalf. He lives! Grace, deliverance, new possibilities are inherent in the promise of Christmas and Easter.

Epiphany and Trinity are seasons which can give expression to our response. Our ethical response, our covenant, and the community of faith are expressions of our answer to the claim of God on our lives. The family experiencing grace finds life freer; what might be mere endless activities can become relationships of substance. These seasons, intentionally viewed, provide signposts through the year on the road to lived-out discipleship.

This model may help illustrate the intent of the seasons:

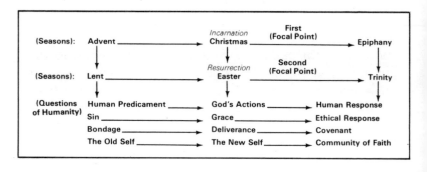

(From Thomas Oden's "Rhythm of the Celebrating Community")

advent

advent

The term "advent" has its root definition in a Latin word which means "coming" or "arrival." Its history goes back to the fifth and sixth century at which time it was celebrated for a longer period. Although Advent is recognized in many churches which have highly developed liturgical observances, in the past century it has come to be appreciated as a special way of anticipating the true meaning of Christmas as the celebration of the Incarnate Lord who has come into the life of persons and comes again and again.

Some traditions which have developed out of the Advent celebration occurred as the institutional church observed the four Sundays before Christmas in particular ways. One aspect of Advent is the recognition that we are separated from God and our fellow human beings; the other is that we have been reconciled to God and humanity through the advent of Christ in the history of the world. These two melodies provide a counterpoint in the music of the Christmas season. We look forward to his "coming" by remembering in special ways during the Advent season.

Some of the traditions which have developed include the Advent wreath, the Advent calendar, special Advent plays. Families often develop customs which are carried through succeeding generations. In some countries the Advent customs are as important to children as are the Christmas observances.

Making an Advent wreath is one activity in which families can symbolically participate in the expectant spirit of Christmastime. The wreath can be made of evergreens—real or artificial. (If greenery is real, it should not be allowed to dry out and become a fire hazard.) The wreath has four candles equal distances apart; sometimes there is also a center candle representing the gift of Jesus, "the light of the world." At the beginning of each week of Advent another candle is lit until on Christmas Eve all four candles are burning, at which time the center one may be lit. For many families the Advent wreath is part of the meal celebration each evening. Some meet just before bedtime in a darkened room and share in the lighting of the wreath.

One family used the wreath at breakfast time each day of the pre-Christmas season. Accompanying the lighting of candles was the reading of a hymn, scripture, or prayer; this was given to the reader on the preceding night to insure familiarity with the words. It is interesting to note that in some sections of Europe the person who is named John or Joan is allowed to light the candles first because the gospel of John speaks of Jesus as the Light of the world.

In Hungary wheat seeds are planted in a small flowerpot on December 13. Kept in a moderately warm room and watered daily, they sprout by Christmas Eve. Children can share the joy of the sprouting wheat. Jesus spoke of his message as "the bread of life." Perhaps your family can talk about the significance of the growing wheat and what it represents.

Another Advent custom is preparing the manger. This originated in France but is practiced today in many countries. Each evening the children bring a piece of straw representing some deed of kindness performed that day. They place the straw in the crib. Then on Christmas Eve when the infant is placed in the crèche, the crib is ready.

Many families have found that the use of the crèche enriches the festivities of Advent for very young children. If your family has a "manger scene," try to have one which can be handled by young children. One mother took time to teach her two-year-old all the different creatures represented in the manger scene. The child played most of the day, murmuring the names of the different animals. That evening when his father came home he took his hand and led him over to the crèche. "That's a lambie," the child said. "That's a cow. That's a sheep. That's a shepherd. That's Mary and the baby Jesus. And that," he said pointing to the figure standing by Mary, "is Jofus—Jofus Christ." This story has been told in the family for nearly twenty years now. It is one of the treasured memories of Advent.

Advent calendars, which originated in Germany, are available in nearly every country now. They feature a scene with windows numbered for the twenty-four days before Christmas. Behind the window for December 24 is always the nativity scene. Small children love the mystery and excitement of these calendars.

The Advent season looks backward and forward

—back to the Creation and forward to the New Creation. In most traditions the Christian year begins with the first Sunday in Advent. Although Easter is an older celebration than Christmas, the addition of other times of celebration has made the Christian year particularly meaningful. There is a drama taking place from Advent on. We wait and hope, and hope comes in our midst. This is celebrated and shared with the world; then come sorrow, death, and resurrection. Hope is restored, and we share anew with the world.

There is change taking place all around us and within our own family circle. The *advent*ure of life together under God is filled with hope and risk. When the word "adventure" is used, we may think of an exciting, unknown, undetermined journey filled with possibilities. Advent is the beginning of such a journey. New situations await us in the coming year. We face the journey into the unknown in faith.

Families can begin a year of intentional celebration by developing some meaningful experiences together starting with Advent.

a time of waiting
(A Service for Advent)

This service may be held during the first of Advent. It may develop out of your family's concern to fill the pre-Christmas season with joy and celebration instead of the usual frantic hassles associated with things-to-do before Christmas Eve. Provide sheets of paper and pencils for each member of the family. This service may begin by lighting the first candle on the Advent wreath and a prayer such as the following:

Prayer   (by a member of the family): God, we want to learn how to wait. We want to savor the time we have as a family. We want to be creative in our relationships. Teach us to wait upon you. In the name of Christ. Amen.

Father: I confess that December is full of so many activities that sometimes I am tired by Christmas.

Mother: I confess that I have lists and lists of things to do and little time to really appreciate the joy of the coming season.

Child: I confess that I am sometimes more interested in what I'm getting for Christmas than in what I am giving to others.

Child: I confess that I wish Christmas was already here!

34

A member of the family: God has heard our attitudes
                          and loves us even while we do not love
                          others. Thank God for his grace!

A parent then explains to the family that the paper sheets are before the members of the family so that each person can record all the different activities that are part of the coming season. Time is allowed for each person to make his or her list. When the lists are made a large list is begun of some of the common concerns such as "visit to Grandma's," "church dinner," "Christmas shopping." Then the family considers the possibility of combining some of the concerns.

Perhaps instead of the parents sending out enormous numbers of Christmas cards, each person will write brief notes to friends in other parts of the country and world, and persons at church and in the neighborhood will receive a special personal greeting.

Perhaps persons who need to be remembered, such as friends who are old or in rest homes, would be more appreciative of a visit around the first of the year when they are not being bombarded with token visits. Perhaps gift wrapping and buying have been too exhausting. Members of the family may need to be supportive of each other during this time. Maybe one or two could shop one evening while other members of the family carry the responsibilities of that person in the home.

As the family works together on concerns, time may be taken to share ideas of ways to make waiting together more meaningful. This will be an excellent time for the parents to share with the children memories of the time before each child was born.

Waiting for the birth of a child is a special time in family life. Children usually love to have these stories told and retold.

There is a song entitled "The Greatest Discovery" recorded by Elton John. In the song the poet-singer chronicles his memory of the birth of his younger brother. A family with teen-agers discovered the recording and that evening invited their parents into the living room. In hushed tones they stated, "This is a song you all have to hear. You'll love it!" The last line is "This is your brand-new brother." The song has a haunting melody. As the last notes ended the older children began to share memories of when the youngest child was born. Then the family spent a meaningful time remembering the birth of each of the children. It was most appropriate to end with a prayer of thanksgiving for the privilege of living together as a family under God.

lιfє that ιscomιnɢ

(A Service for Advent)

This service of worship uses the Hungarian tradition of planting wheat seeds. It should be held near the second Sunday of Advent. In Hungary the seeds are planted about December 15 so that they will sprout by Christmas Eve. You will want to plant them as part of the celebration of worship. The earth should be soft and moist. You may buy the seeds at a granary or a seed store. A small cardboard carton may be used, or you may want to plant them in a special vase that can be used each Christmas. Choose a vase that has

adequate drainage, since the seeds will need watering. After the family gathers together, one of the group tells of this Hungarian tradition which symbolizes the way God gives life meaning through Christ. As these seeds germinate and sprout the family is reminded of the scripture, "I am the bread of life; he that cometh to me shall never hunger; and he that believeth on me shall never thirst" (John 6:35). The sixth chapter of John contains references to Jesus as the "bread of life."

We may not completely understand this. We know there are people who are followers of Jesus who suffer and are hungry, but he promises in this scripture that even in the midst of loneliness and pain, life can have meaning.

Bread is a food shared throughout the world. It provides energy. Just as the wheat seeds are planted and receive nourishment in the soil and grow into wheat, so do we receive nourishment from the bread. Let us plant the seeds of wheat, remembering that during the Advent season we celebrate that which is going to happen—Christmas. We celebrate now the wheat which will grow in this soil.

Family member   (*as he or she places the seed in the soil*): I give thanks to God for the life in this seed.

Family member   (*doing the same*): I give thanks to God for the soil in which life already is waiting.

Family member: I give thanks to God for our family which shares the promise of Jesus that our life will continue.

Family member: I give thanks to God for his presence with us now. Amen.

WE CELEBRATE ADVENT

Leader: Advent means *coming*. Whose coming do we celebrate?

Family members: We celebrate the coming of the Lord.

1st voice: We celebrate the coming of God into the life of all persons in Christ.

2nd voice: We celebrate the coming of Christ in our lives today through the concern and love of others.

1st voice: We celebrate the Lord coming to us in the human need of other people.

Leader: Lord, when did we see you hungry and feed you?

When did we see you thirsty and give you a drink?

When did we see you naked and give you some clothes?

When were you sick? When did we visit you?

When were you in prison? When did we come to see you?

Family together: When you do any of these things for anyone—great or small, you are doing them for me.

(Based on Matt. 25:34-41 I.V.)

1st voice: We celebrate God's coming to us today.
2nd voice: We celebrate his coming in our midst.
Family together: We celebrate the coming of the Lord.
(The family may find special appreciation in sharing this hymn.)

Battle Hymn of the Republic Irregular with Refrain

M. ♩ 100

Julia Ward Howe, 1819-1910

William Steffe, 1852

1. Mine eyes have seen the glo - ry of the com - ing of the Lord;
2. I have seen him in the watch-fires of a hun-dred cir - cling camps;
3. He has sound-ed forth the trum-pet that shall nev - er call re-treat;
4. In the beau-ty of the lil - ies Christ was born a-cross the sea,

He is tram-pling out the vint-age where the grapes of wrath are stored;
They have build-ed him an al - tar in the eve-ning dews and damps;
He is sift-ing out the hearts of men be-fore his judg-ment seat;
With a glo - ry in his bos-om that trans-fig-ures you and me;

He hath loosed the fate - ful light - ning of his ter - ri - ble swift sword;
I can read his right - eous sen - tence by the dim and flar - ing lamps,
O be swift, my soul, to an - swer him; be ju - bi - lant, my feet!
As he died to make men ho - ly, let us die to make men free,

REFRAIN

His truth is march - ing on.
His day is march - ing on.
Our God is march - ing on.
While God is march - ing on.

Glo - ry, glo - ry, hal - le - lu - jah!

Glo - ry, glo - ry, hal - le - lu - jah! Glo - ry, glo - ry,

hal - le - lu - jah! His truth is march - ing on.

41

chRistmas eve seRvice

A member of the family (*lighting the first candle*): This candle tells us that God keeps his promises. He promised persons that he would never leave them. His gift of Jesus is the way he kept that promise.

Another member of the family (*lighting second candle*]: This candle tells us that Jesus has shown us how to love God and to love one another.

Another member of the family (*lighting third candle*): This candle reminds us that Jesus helps us see ways of sharing our lives with others.

Another member of the family (*lighting fourth candle*]: This candle reminds us that when we give gifts to others to celebrate Christmas we are remembering his great gift to us.

A member of the family reads John 1:1-14.

Family sings together No. 146 from *The Hymnal*, "Newborn of God."

Father: What can we say to God on this joyful night?

Family: Thank you, God, for your great gift.

Mother: What can we bring to God to show our thanks?

Family: We bring our lives as an offering.

Child: What has God said to us in this time together?

Family: God has spoken in a person—Jesus. He has told us that he loves us just as we are at this very moment. He has said to us, "You are loved. You are accepted."

Child: What then do we say to each other at this moment?

Family members turn to face each other saying: God loves you. I love you.

All: Amen.

christmas

chRistmas

Although Easter was celebrated in the first century Christian church, the observance of the birthday memory of the Lord Jesus was not officially established until probably sometime in the fourth century. Christmas is a holiday which bears witness of the redeeming life of Christ. What once was a pagan holiday has been transformed into a worldwide celebration of love and peace, observed by non-Christians as well as followers of the risen Lord. Christmas was introduced into the church, according to some scholars, to crowd out the corrupt celebrations of the winter solstice celebrated by the Romans. From the time of Emperor Aurelian (274) the Romans had honored the sun god (Sol Invictus: the Unconquered Sun) on December 25.

In the early Christian church great care was taken to emphasize the solemnity of the celebration. It was originally called "Christ's Mass." The term Christmas probably came into use during the twentieth century.

Christmas has undergone many changes in the centuries since its introduction into the Christian calendar. There was always the concern that it not take on the character of the pagan festivals being held at the same time. With the reformation in the sixteenth century a great change occurred in the emphasis on the ritualism of the festival. Although some of the reformed churches maintained a deep devotion to the memory of the Christ

46

Child, followers of the Puritan movement resisted Christmas because they felt it was considered more important than the Sabbath.

The Puritans outlawed Christmas in England when they achieved political power. However, the people paid little attention to this. The issue grew into relative importance, and during the 1640's persons were arrested, riots occurred, and Christmas—the festival of peace—was celebrated with anger and violence. Gradually, the external observance of Christmas was extinguished, and it became a common workday in England. Then in 1660, with the restoration of the monarchy, Christmas became a holiday again. However, in the homes and communities a new dimension of feasting and celebration had come. Christmas, while still pagan in the minds of the austere Pilgrims, was a season of special meaning to believer and nonbeliever. It began a traditional time for goodwill and generosity. It took on special meaning for families. Today, although the commercialized, secularized aspect is disturbing, Christmas continues to be a reminder of the marvelous gift of God in his Son Jesus. Despite the hypocrisy of the situation, for a twenty-four-hour period many people are kind even to those they ignore during other times of the year. It is as though Christmas elicits from them the finest and best that they are.

Some of the customs associated with Christmas have their rootage in pre-Christian times. Others are part of the history of those who saw symbolically in their world reminders of God's love. The Romans gave presents at their winter celebrations, and Christians have continued the custom in recognition of God's gift of his Son. From Germany came the custom of using the evergreen tree as a symbol of everlasting life. The Druids offered mistletoe which they believed had healing power; Christians accepted it as a symbol of the Christ who was "the healing of the nations." From England came the legend that holly represented the blood-marked crown of thorns. The yule log originated in Scandinavia where its burning represented a way to destroy past hatreds and distrusts. Firecrackers, which came from China, are used in South America as part of the Christmas celebration.

Christmas is rich in legend and symbol—bells, candles, St. Nicholas, lights, stockings, trees, animals. The day offers abundant opportunity to remember a common story. A family with four children gathered one Christmas Eve to share in Christmas worship. The father had chosen the traditional story from Luke . . . but this Christmas was very special. One of the older boys had created a beautiful gift for his father. He had hand-tooled a leather briefcase. The children were eager to open gifts so the father could receive this special surprise. As the family gathered, the father agreed that for the first time Christmas gifts would be opened early—one minute after midnight. As the children (all junior high age or older) sat around the table, the parents suggested that they share memories of Christmases past. As each person related some special memory of a past Christmas, all members of the family grew closer. They were sharing their common history, and it held great meaning.

Then each was asked to state something he or she wished for the moment. This was "Christmas present." The contemporary point in the family history would be enriched by these statements. One of the younger children wished he could fly. This evoked some delightful conversation. The eldest son wished to be reconciled with two of his friends. When the daughter, who had not shared a wish, was asked what she wanted, she said quietly, "I don't think I can share it." Suddenly her older brother leaped up and called the family to the living room. "Come on, you guys. I have a great idea." He had them get in a circle with their arms around each other. "Now, put your heads together," he instructed. "Be sure your head is touching someone else's. Now, think of that person. Remember something you have done together. Think until you can see that person in your mind."

A spirit of intimacy and concern came into the circle. At this point, the innovator said, "Okay, sis, we are all supporting you now. You can tell us what you wish."

In a small, tight voice, she whispered, "I wish I made friends more easily." The brother at this point squeezed his sister tightly. The family moved back around the table. There was a comfortable quiet. No one spoke. The girl was visibly moved. She had shared her deepest secret. She had left herself vulnerable.

At this point her brother, who for years had teased her, went to her and held her in his arms.

The father reached for the Scriptures. "I usually read from Luke," he said, "but tonight our Christmas Scripture is found in the second chapter of Corinthians: 'When anyone is united to Christ, there is a new world; the old order has gone, and a new order has already begun. From first to last this has been the work of God. He has reconciled us men to himself through Christ, and he has enlisted us in this service of reconciliation. What I mean is, that God was in Christ, reconciling the world to himself, no longer holding men's misdeeds against them, and that he has entrusted us with the message of reconciliation. We come therefore as Christ's ambassadors.' "

Indeed, for this family the word of reconciliation had been made flesh in the lives of its members on Christmas Eve. The day meant more than gifts wrapped in paper under a tree. It was the gift of the Holy Spirit which enabled persons to see with new understanding and to be truly reconciled to one another.

Whatever traditions have given your family an opportunity to draw near to each other and to God bear sustaining. But leave yourself open to new possibilities. Christmas is symbolic of the opportunity God gives for newness in life each day.

a family drama at christmas

In many homes the Christmas story has been enacted by the children through the years. One mother told about her two grown sons enlisting neighbor children to come in and "act out Christmas." This is one way of sharing at Christmastime—invite neighbor children to share the Christmas story with you.

Another way is to put out some towels and headbands and let every member of the family "dress up" to participate in the story as recorded in Luke or Matthew.

Here are some guidelines. Perhaps the tradition in your family may be that the father reads the Christmas story from Matthew or Luke. This year allow one of the younger children just achieving the exciting skill of reading to practice reading the story and to serve in the role of narrator. The parts for the drama are unlimited. Choose whichever Christmas story is a favorite in your family. Tradition has said that there were three wise men, but the nativity story itself deals with a mother, father, baby, animals, and shepherds. There are other characters; you may want to act out the entire story, but try to include adults in roles which children have usually played. Use bathrobes, sheets, or whatever props help create a mood. Allow each person to take a part. Another guideline is to remember that you are recalling a beloved story which has given meaning to your life. Do not stay tied to the Scripture record. A church school teacher recalls that one of the most meaningful nativity pageants included the performance of a six-year-old girl who was portraying Mary, the mother of Jesus. As the curtains opened, she looked out at the audience and said, "You must please be quiet. Baby Jesus is sleeping." Then, unrehearsed, she got up, placed the baby in the manger, and said (again to the audience), "I've got to fix something to eat. The shepherds are coming soon and Jesus wouldn't want them to be hungry." This certainly was not in the script, but it reflected the kind of caring this young child had learned. The congregation was confronted with a new appreciation for the scripture, "When I was hungry, you fed me."

Allow this experience in your family to be a dramatization of a cherished story which has enriched your life. If the adults can participate freely, the story will have even greater meaning for the children.

You may want to end the drama by singing a familiar carol. You may even want to learn a new carol. Here is a favorite one for young children: "Mary Had a Baby."

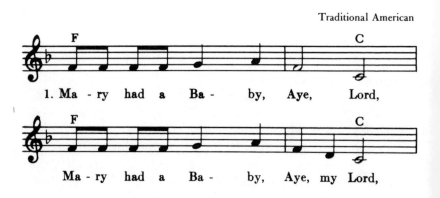

Traditional American

1. Ma - ry had a Ba - by, Aye, Lord,

Ma - ry had a Ba - by, Aye, my Lord,

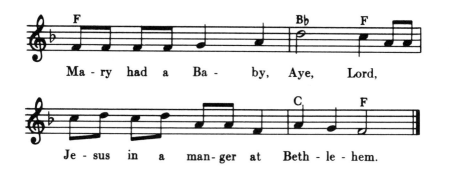

Ma - ry had a Ba - by, Aye, Lord,

Je - sus in a man- ger at Beth - le - hem.

What did she name Him
She named the baby Jesus.
Where was He born?
Born in a manger.
Wisemen came to see him.

53

a post-christmas celebration

The week after Christmas is often a letdown for families. Visitors leave, the excitement is gone, and joy of the festivities is difficult to sustain.

The week between Christmas Day and Epiphany can be a good time for the family to experience a sense of quiet joy. This may be projected by the use of an old symbol of the nativity, the daisy. No one knows when the daisy was first used to symbolize the innocence of the newborn Christ, but it is thought that all white flowers have been used through the centuries to signify the purity and freshness of the infant Jesus.

For this celebration you will need some white poster or construction paper, glue, scissors, and magic marking pens. A pattern of daisy petals will be helpful. In the center of each person's daisy write words such as "Christmas every day means" or "Christmas through the year means" or "Christmas lived is." The daisy center may be prepared in advance of the gathering of the family. Each member will be given a center as the family gathers. For a song to bring the family together, you may want to use selected passages of "O Little Town of Bethlehem." The following stanzas fit the occasion:

How silently, how silently, the wondrous gift is given.
So God imparts to human hearts the blessings of his heaven.
No ear may hear his coming, but in this world of sin,
Where meek souls will receive him still the dear Christ enters in.

O Holy Child of Bethlehem, descend to us, we pray;
Cast out our sin and enter in, be born in us today.
We hear the Christmas angels the great glad tidings tell;
O come to us, abide with us, our Lord Immanuel!

A Litany for Families

Leader: We come to continue our celebration.

All: We thank God for the gift of Christ.

Leader: We come to renew our Christmas wonder.

All: We thank God for the gift of Christ.

Leader: In the offering of ourselves to others we continue our celebration.

All: We thank God for the gift of Christ.

After the family members have shared the litany, the leader explains the purpose of the daisy center. Then the supplies are made available and the members of the family are invited to write specific activities on the petals of the daisies. For instance, a girl may get a center with "Christmas every day means" written on it. On the petals she may write "remembering to write Grandma each week," "Learning to listen to other members of the family," "helping Sandy with her math," "practicing piano cheerfully," "trying to speak Spanish with Mrs. Romez," "really caring about other people." These petals are attached with glue to the center of her daisy, which is then placed with the others on a bulletin board in the family room. The daisies might be glued to sticks and placed in a large vase; always they should be prominently displayed. The daisies are visual reminders of ways to make Christmas a year-around reality.

epiphany

epiphany

The meaning of Epiphany is "manifestation." This season of the Christian year offers the family a rich opportunity to celebrate the revelation of God to the world in Jesus Christ. Celebrated on January 6, in some cultures, it is thought to be the Eastern version of the Western tradition of Christmas. However, this is a limited understanding of this season. Epiphany conveys primarily the manifestations of God to the world through Jesus Christ.

Epiphany was celebrated some time before the fourth century when Christmas became a Christian festival. The birth and baptism of Jesus were commemorated in this season. In the last quarter of the fourth century Epiphany was named the Holy Day of Lights and included the celebration of the adoration of the Magi. The "Twelfth Day," as Epiphany came to be known, is celebrated by some cultures as a day of present giving (this is true in Spain and South America). Just as the Scriptures record the gifts of gold, frankincense, and myrrh, so do children anticipate gifts received at the home of grandparents.

In Austria, Germany, France, England, and parts of Canada the tradition of the festival of the "King's Cake" was celebrated. This cake was baked on Epiphany in honor of the Magi and eaten at a special party. Often a coin was put in the dough, and the person who found it was the "king." In some of the countries a bean and pea were baked in the cake, making the respective finders "king" and "queen" of the celebration.

The Magi theme developed from the single sentence in the scripture, "There came wise men from the east." But the tradition has developed through the centuries until today some children are amazed that they cannot find the scripture about the Three Kings of the Orient or a reference to Gaspar, Melchior, Balthasar. Legends and traditions developed through the centuries can help families understand the tremendous impact of the life of God in the midst of human experience. The central truth inherent in the season of Epiphany is that God took upon himself flesh. The family members can use the four to nine Sundays after Christmas as a time of reexamining what the action of God means to them. The response can be through specific action, and it can also be in a renewed appreciation for what it means to live under God today.

fOR the New YeAR

Now faith is the assurance of *things hoped for*, the conviction of things not seen. . . . By faith Abraham obeyed when he was called out to a place where he was to receive as an inheritance; and *he went out, not knowing where he was to go.* By faith he sojourned in the land of promise, as in a foreign land. . . . *For he looked* forward to the city which has foundations, whose builder and maker is God.

The family might try to understand what this scripture means by discussing several questions:

1. What are some things I hope for? (Each member responds to this.)
2. Do I know for sure what will happen each day? (Perhaps some of the surprises which have been part of the experiences of members of the family can be shared.)
3. What do I look forward to? (This might be asked: "What do I expect to happen in my life today, next week, next year?")

Following this discussion the leader (who may be one of the older children rather than a parent) may want to read the scripture again. A new year is beginning. The person filled with hope faces a new year expectantly. To live in faith is to trust in God and to be willing to risk. What risks will the family be willing to take this year? (Some suggestions for possible risk: extending the circle of friendship to include persons who are different; recording priorities and assuming responsibility for others less fortunate; participating actively in the political issues of the community and nation; engaging in more open and honest relationships within the home and with others.)

we face a brand-new year

(This service can be used during the second week of Epiphany if the family wishes.)

Leader: I will praise God.
All: I will praise God every day.
Leader: Great is the Lord and greatly to be praised.
All: One generation shall praise the works of God to another.
Leader: We shall praise the works of God to each other.
All: And declare his mighty acts.
(Paraphrase of Psalm 145:1-4)

One family always uses the first week of the new year to record important changes. A record is kept on the doorjamb in the kitchen of the physical growth of all members of the family since they have lived in the house. This one strip of wood has never been repainted. The weight of each individual at the time of measuring is also recorded.

After this is done, all of them gather back at the kitchen or dining room table where sheets of paper and pencils are made available, and each one is asked to share the differences in height or weight with other members of the family. Then the individuals write or draw something which indicates some aspect of change which he or she hopes to realize in the coming year. (One of the younger boys drew a picture of himself as a six-foot-six basketball star. This picture was treasured through the years.) The pictures or statements are then placed on the bulletin board (or prayer board) to serve as reminders of the willingness to change and grow together. (One family who participated in this exercise agreed to sustain the oldest son who was overweight. He decided when he recorded his weight gain to begin to exercise discipline in his eating habits. This provided a chance for others in the family to pledge support for him as he began a new diet. Their love and concern made the change in his eating habits possible.)

Following the sharing of the commitment to change, the family members join hands. One person offers a brief prayer affirming the presence of God in the midst of change and offering members of the family as agents of change for the sake of His kingdom.

sanò canòles for epiphany

Epiphany, the season of light, is celebrated by Christians as a reminder that Christ, the Light of the world, lived and loved on behalf of all persons everywhere. In some countries this season is called the Feast of the Lights.

A delightful family activity may be making sand candles. These can be placed in an appropriate setting and a time of worship set aside in which they are lit.

Materials need to be placed in a specific work area. Each member of the family may choose a particular shaped container for his or her candle. One container

is needed per candle (margarine tubs, tin cans, cottage cheese cartons, etc., may be used). Each container should be half full of sand which is quite damp but not "soupy." The sand should hold its shape when packed. Wicking should be tied to sticks or pencils. This will be placed over the top of the container after the wax has been poured in. The wicking should have weights tied to each piece (old screws, nuts, washers).

Begin by heating wax in a large can placed in a pan of hot water to form a double boiler. (A three-pound shortening can is good for this project.) Put newspapers and drop cloths on the floor to protect it from sand and wax. Now fill the containers half full of sand wet enough to pack. Shape the sand around the entire inside of the container. At this point in the process you may want to make designs in the sand (a cross, a fish, a name). If you want to have feet on the candle, be certain that you make three holes that reach all the way to the bottom of the container. If the feet are uneven the candle will tip over. Pour the hot wax in the molded sand. Drop the weighted wick in the center of the mold and place the straw, stick, or pencil to which the wick is tied across the top of the container.

When the wax hardens remove the candle from the container and brush off excess sand.

After the family members have made candles, plan a time when the candles will be put in a setting where they can be lit. Then, if it is desirable, a time of worship may be planned.

You may want to do something like this:

Leader: It is the season of Epiphany. Translated from Greek, Epiphany can mean "a shining upon." Let us give thanks for the ways in which God has graced our life together as a family.

Family member: I have found God present in our Christmas celebration.

Family member: I have found God present in our sharing together.

Leader: God has shone upon us as we have remembered his gift to us of his Son, Jesus.

Family member: I have found God present in...

[At this point members of the family share memories of times during the season when they have experienced a sense of God's presence.]

Leader: We thank God for Christ Jesus, the Light of the world.

Family together: We light our candles to remember God's love for us.
We light our candles to remind us to love others.

(Then each person lights the candle he or she made.)

This time together can be most meaningful if the members of the family meet in a nearly darkened room. If persons read the preceding material, a flashlight may be needed. However, the simplicity of this time is important. Perhaps the service can be shared without any specific words being read.

we reflect...the lord

This time of sharing may be most appropriate at the table following a meal. Under each person's plate, place a tiny pocket-size mirror. On the back of the mirror have the following scripture printed on a piece of paper and glued to the mirror:

...Because for us there is no veil over the face, we all reflect as a mirror the splendor of the Lord; thus we are transfigured into his likeness, from splendor to splendor; such is the influence of the Lord who is Spirit.

You may want to spend a moment talking about the scripture. There may be particular people who have reflected the "splendor of the Lord" to your family. There may be relatives such as a grandmother or uncle whose faith has been a strength for others. Perhaps a member of the congregation has exemplified courage and faith. This would be an excellent time to express appreciation for these people.

Now family members hold the mirrors up and look into them. One member of the family may want to read this prayer:

Sometimes, God, when I look at my image I am ashamed of myself. I know that I do things that are wrong. I do not like to look at myself sometimes. But now, I look in the mirror and see me. I know that I can reflect your image to others. Now, God, I give thanks for myself. I commit myself to reflecting the image of me that is indeed the image of you. In the name of Jesus, whose image made it possible for us to know the depths of your love, amen.

Now, each member of the family tells one way in which he/she feels that God's life may be seen through him/her in the coming week.

Following this, the family may join hands and sing "They'll Know We Are Christians by Our Love."

valentine's day

There is a theory that initially Valentine's Day was a pagan festival, Lupercalia, held around the middle of February. In an attempt to Christianize the celebration the day was named in honor of a third century priest who was clubbed and beheaded on Valentine's Day. There are other legends about the origin of St. Valentine's Day. The celebration is an established custom in many countries. It is important then to provide a setting in which the tradition of expressing love which is associated with this holiday can be experienced in a creative way.

It may be appropriate to read the first part of *The Velveteen Rabbit* (or you may want to read the entire book or use the tape by Louise Wrigley). Another excellent reading is found on pages 64-71 of *The Little Prince*. Following this members of the family can share together in reading I Corinthians 13:1-7:

Voice 1: I may be able to speak the languages of men and even of angels, but if I have not love, my speech is no more than a noisy gong or a clanging bell.

Voice 2: I may have the gift of inspired preaching; I may have all knowledge and understand all secrets; I may have all the faith needed to move mountains—but if I have not love, I am nothing.

Voice 3: I may give away everything I have and even give up my body to be burned—but if I have not love, it does me no good.

Voice 1: Love is patient and kind;

Voice 2: Love is not jealous, or conceited, or proud;

Voice 3: Love is not ill-mannered, or selfish, or irritable;

Voice 1: Love does not keep a record of wrongs;

Voice 2: Love is not happy with evil, but is happy with the truth.

Voice 3: Love never gives up: its faith, hope, and patience never fails.

All: Love is eternal.

Voice 1: Our lives are claimed by those who love us.

Voice 2: To love is to belong to others.

Voice 3: Yet love frees us to be ourselves—real and authentic.

All: Empower us to love each other and others, God. Amen.

the chain of love

The third Sunday in February is known as Brotherhood Sunday and introduces Brotherhood Week in many Christian communities. It may be appropriate to consider a special time in the family for a similar observance. Perhaps rather than calling this time a celebration of brotherhood, it might be called a "Celebration of Oneness." This will allow women in the family to feel they are being seen as whole persons.

The symbol for this gathering might be the material for a paper chain, such as those made at Christmas. Strips of paper, scissors, and glue will be needed. The parents are in the best position to facilitate this gathered time, since the family began with them.

Before the children arrive the mother and father may want to have completed the part of the chain containing the names of great-grandparents, great-aunts, great-uncles, grandparents, uncles, aunts, and cousins written on individual links. Then they may lead the worship in the following manner:

Father: Who are we who gather here at this moment?

Mother: We are the children of God. We are children of parents and grandparents.

All: We are members of a family.

Father: I remember when I was very young, my mother [or father] told me this story of when she [or he] was very young. (At this point the father recalls a story from his childhood which has been meaningful to him through the years.)

Mother: I remember a story I heard as a child about something that meant a great deal to my parents. (Mother then shares the story.)

Father: The chain that is already linked together represents family members who have gone before us. There are many people about whom we know nothing who have helped make us a family.

Mother: But they are part of who we are now.

All: We are members of a large family.

(The children are now given opportunity to share memories of their relatives.)

Each family member is then instructed to write his or her name on a strip of the paper and add it to the chain.

At this point, the father writes the name of someone who is not related to him in any way but to whom he feels a sense of relationship. Perhaps naming someone in another country or from another culture would be particularly meaningful. The mother does this also. Then they add these pieces of paper to the chain containing the names of persons who have given them a greater appreciation of life.

(The children are also given opportunity to participate in this way. They may print the name of any person they feel has enriched their lives.)

Mother: We have family names on our chain. We have names of those to whom we are related only by the binding power of love.

Father: But our chain can keep growing. We will not
          consider it finished.

All: We are members of God's family on earth—all of
        his creation.

(One of the children then reads the following
scripture.)

This is the message you heard from the very beginning that we
must love one another.

Our love should not be just words and talk; it must be true love,
which shows itself in action.

—I John 3:11 and 18 (Phillips).

All: We are sent forth to be links in a chain of love
        which shows itself in action.

pre-lenten

a mealtime moment
of celebration

This is another opportunity to share something more than simply a prayer of thanks for the food. This liturgy may be used with friends, or you may want to use it at family mealtime when there are no guests present.

Leader: Before breaking bread together let us share our joy with each other.

Each person then responds individually to the statement:

Today I have reason to celebrate. . . .

When each has spoken, the following is shared:

Leader: God calls us together to celebrate the ties that bind us to each other.

All: He calls us now in love.

Leader: We have shared joyful memories tonight. Not all memories are joyful, but we thank God for the condition of our lives.

All: God gives us life.

Leader: We shall now break bread together, thankful for abundance, but concerned about those who have not.

All: God calls us to share his life and love.

the good news

The newspapers should be saved for a week for this worship activity. As the family gathers, give each member a portion of the paper, then explain that the first part of this time together will be spent looking for articles or illustrations of the broken condition of humanity. There are many stories which evoke sorrow and pain. Allow a few minutes for finding these articles. Now ask everyone to share the reason for these broken conditions.

Next, using the same papers, look for signs of hope or evidence of God at work in the world. After a few minutes ask each to share what he/she has found and to suggest ways in which the family may join God in his work in the particular area about which the article is written.

For a sending forth, the following may be used:

Voice 1: We live in a world that is bleeding and broken.

All: We live in God's world.

Voice 2: We live in a world that is promising and hopeful.

All: We live in God's world.

Voice 1: Who will go to serve the needs of God's world?

Voice 2: Who will go to bring his good news?

All: All are called according to the gifts of God unto them.
We are called.
We will go.

love them now

A new hymn can enrich the life of any group. This is true of the family. One meaningful way to appreciate a hymn is to see its relevance to the immediate situation. "Love Them Now" offers an opportunity for persons in the family to confront the alienation they feel toward some people. The confession of this separation can be stated, and pardon can be granted by someone in the circle of the family or by the corporate group. The song can in this way become the word of God to members of the family, sending them forth to truly love others "now."

You may want to ask someone in the family who sings well to share this song first as a solo. If not, then spend some time as a group learning the song.

Following this sharing, perhaps the members of the family can think of specific ways in which they can offer love to lonely, strange, peculiar people. What are the attitudes that can reconcile those who "are hard to get along with, who demand and hate and tear down ev'ry one"? In what particular ways can parents and children see one another as "hungry, needing people" and treat each with understanding?

After this discussion, you may want to have someone read the following scripture:

Leader: Beloved, let us love one another
All: For love is of God.
Leader: Everyone that loves is born of God and knows God.
All: For love is of God.
Leader: And this commandment have we: We who love God must love others.
All: For love is of God.

(Paraphrase of I John 4:7, 21.)

LOVE THEM NOW

Dedicated to Lucille Sexton

RICHARD AVERY
DONALD MARSH

lent

Lent

The need to prepare for every significant religious occasion is part of Jewish tradition. This concern has been continued by Christians. Easter, almost from the beginning of its observance with the Christians of the first century, was a season rather than a single day. The length of the season had developed into a Holy Week by the third century. The pre-Easter season was finally extended to forty days by the Nicene council.

The English meaning of the word is "spring," but this does not convey the disciplines of fasting and prayer that have been observed for centuries during this period of time. When Lent was developed, Good Friday as a distinctive commemoration of the Passion did not exist. Lent became the observance which tied the people to Easter with a sense of repentance and expectation.

In the early Christian church, baptismal services usually were held only once a year—at Easter time. The Lenten period of preparation may have grown out of this period of preparation and training of candidates. Different scholars suggest biblical backgrounds for the forty days of Lent. Some suggest that it symbolizes the time Moses spent on Mount Sinai, or the forty years of wandering in the wilderness, or the forty days of Jesus' temptation, or his forty hours in the tomb.

Catholics still observe Lent with special disciplines, beginning with Ash Wednesday, the first day of the season. Fasting plays an important part in this ritual. During the Reformation, some of the Protestant churches retained the Lenten fast for a time. After about 1660 the Lenten laws were generally neglected in England until 1863 when Parliament finally repealed them. Many Christians have found the discipline of fasting and prayer prior to Easter to be a meaningful expression of faith. While the Restoration calendar has never included Lent as an officially designated time, in many congregations pre-Easter services and activities are planned. Lent can be particularly meaningful if viewed as a time for self-examination in which families come to understand some of their estrangement from God and look forward to the celebration of the death and resurrection of Christ.

Ancient customs practiced in other countries might be interesting and enriching for present-day families to share. The middle of the Lenten season (the fourth Sunday) is considered a day of joy within the mourning season. The Roman church observes this with great ritual. Toward the end of the Middle Ages in Protestant England an interesting custom developed. The fourth Sunday of Lent became known as "Mothering Sunday." Young boys and girls who worked away from home as apprentices and servants were allowed to go home to visit the church at which they had been baptized (their "mother church"). These were the places where they had learned to worship— the most important places in their experience. They took gifts to the altar. During this same time of remembrance they visited with their families and gave particular attention to their mothers, often presenting flowers and plum cakes. Many of the young people did housework during this weekend as a special way of observing the holiday. An ancient carol in the Oxford Book of Carols is entitled "Mothering Sunday." One cannot help wondering if the American custom of "Mother's Day" has indirect rootage in this celebration.

While "Mothering Sunday" seems dreadfully archaic in an age of mobility, professional women, and emancipated young people, the middle of the season prior to Easter might offer a good opportunity to celebrate individuals in the family as being special to each other. Perhaps designating a time to confess feelings of alienation and resentment could provide the foundation for a family observance of joy. If the purpose of the Lenten season is to emphasize repentance and expectancy, what better way for the family to face Easter than to come together anticipating the reconciliation possible through forgiveness?

Sometimes an experience of estrangement lasts for many days because we are so convinced of the "rightness" of a particular position. The Lenten season points us to the crucifixion in which Christ gave himself completely on our behalf. Self-giving love enables us to see someone else's point of view as having meaning and the new person as having worth. Lent may provide the family with several opportunities to share together in experiences of reconciliation.

a lenten service of confession and reconciliation

An older member of the family should be asked in advance to read the story of Jesus' experience in the garden the night of his betrayal (John 7). Then the story should be shared in the reader's own words. The synopsis might read something like this:

Writers of the Scriptures have recorded that "the night Jesus was captured by the Roman soldiers, he had gone to the garden to pray. There in the quiet setting he had asked God for the strength to carry out the task that was his. Not only had Jesus prayed about his own concerns but he had prayed for his disciples. He prayed that 'they might be one,' even as he and his father were one. The disciples did not always get along well together. They argued over who was the most important and in later years about who should get to hear about Jesus. But Jesus knew they were loved of God even as he was loved. He had prayed that the love he felt for them might be shared."

This is only a suggested way to tell the story. However it is told, the emphasis on the hope that Christ felt in the power of love to draw people into "oneness" should be stressed.

Following the scripture one of the older children may want to read a children's story about reconciliation. Some suggestions are *Bartholomew and the Oobleck, Horton Hears a Who* by Dr. Seuss, or the story of Theodore from the booklet *Balloons Belong in Church* (at the end of this chapter).

Following the story each member of the family might recall some experience in which he or she felt alienated. The incident should be told through the feelings of the person. The offender may not be named. For instance, if eleven-year-old Jack has been angry with seventeen-year-old Mary for accidentally breaking his race car, he is *not* to say, "Mary made me mad when she stepped on my red car." Instead, he might say, "I am very angry because my red car was broken when someone stepped on it." Persons need to learn to practice "claiming their feelings." By sending out "I" messages instead of "you" messages the person will be better able to deal with the problem. It is important that the one who has been hurt be allowed to continue to express how he or she feels. Then the one who is involved in this may feel moved to express regret. It is possible that the "offender" is completely unaware of the offense. (Perhaps Mary didn't know that she stepped on the truck, since it was on the sidewalk and she was hurriedly leaving.)

This period should be more than a "gripe" session. The person who feels estrangement should be helped to realize his or her responsibility for the situation.

Following this time of sharing, a short litany may be read:

Individual: God, you have given us a chance to live together, and sometimes we mess it up. We don't like to be responsible for our feelings.

The family in unison: Help us to live in forgiveness
and love.

Individual: We often are more interested in our
own things and concerns and don't even
see or hear the people who live with us
here in our home.

The family in unison: Help us to live in forgiveness
and love.

Individual: Sometimes we are angry. Sometimes
we are stubborn. Sometimes we don't love
anyone—not even ourselves.

The family in unison: Help us to live in forgiveness
and love.

Then all are invited to stand and form a circle with
their arms around each other while one of the group
pronounces a blessing such as the following: "God has
loved us when we were not lovable. He sends us forth
to love each other."

THEODORE

When I was a little boy I had a mama who, most of the time, I
liked. But *sometimes* I didn't like her. Like when she would pop
my hand, or another place! Or when she would holler at me, or
scold me, or not do what I wanted her to, or make me do
something I didn't want to. I, also, had a Teddy Bear named
Theodore. I *always* liked my Teddy Bear because it would never
pop me, or scold me, or make me do things I don't want to do.
Every night, and especially on the nights when I didn't like my
mother, Theodore and I would crawl into bed and we would lie
there hugging each other before we went to sleep. I could always
depend on my Theodore.

But, there's another part to the story. My Theodore had a hairy,
fuzzy, fat, round belly. And what I liked to do before I went to

sleep was to suck my thumb but not just suck my thumb—no—it was so much better to grab a finger full of Theodore's tummy hair and tickle my nose with it while I sucked my thumb. Well, guess what happened. One night when I especially didn't like my mama, I pulled some of Theodore's hair and Theodore ripped wide open! I let out the wildest, loudest scream you ever heard, but Theodore just lay there. Can you guess who came into my room to see what was the matter? It was my mama. And all of a sudden I liked her very much. She held me and dried my tears.

Maybe that helped me learn that even though mamas and daddys and other big people including bosses and loud-mouth fellow workers make you mad sometimes, they also are the ones who can dry your tears, and give you love and make you feel good. Teddy Bears are nice, but people are the only ones who can love you and help you not be afraid and lonely.

———
—The Reverend Richard Spaugh, Chaplain Moravian Academy, *Balloons Belong in Church*, 1973.

the family explores
the possibilities of prayer

In the book, *A Private House of Prayer*, Dr. Leslie Weatherhead suggests that we could view the experience of prayer as a visit to a house. He indicates that the house may be considered to have seven rooms:

1. The room where we affirm the presence of God.
2. The room where we praise, thank, and adore God.
3. The room of confession, unloading, and forgiveness.
4. The room where we receive divine acceptance and promise.
5. The room for purified desire and holy petition.
6. The room where we intercede for others.
7. The room for meditation.

It is possible sometimes that in the prayer life of a person each of the seven rooms may be visited for a period of time. However, most often a person enters only one or two rooms of a house; this is true even in the individual's own home.

Perhaps as a family for one week you can experiment

with each of the rooms. At one of the meals or at a time when all of you are together, plan for each member to share a statement affirming the presence of God. Then on the next day find a time in which you can offer praise or thanksgiving. This can be done in very simple ways. One family begins Monday morning using the modern song, "Here Comes the Sun." The parents arise first and the song is played on the family stereo—with the volume high. The father and mother come to the table first, and as the children come down to breakfast one of the parents greets them with a statement such as "Today I affirm the presence of God as I sense the unfulfilled dreams we each have, as I see the possibilities in the week ahead, and as I live in the hope that the love we share gives to me." Then each member of the family who wishes to do so offers a statement to affirm the presence of God.

The seven rooms may be visited in one week. Prayers may be said in the traditional manner, or you may have—following each person's statement of affirmation—a group response of "Amen," or "So be it," or "It shall be so," or "God go with you today."

we celebrate faith
in a time of fear

The pre-Easter season is an excellent time for the family to share concerns in a setting which may create a sense of hope. Frequently persons carry fears and doubts which seem impossible to mention, yet when these "private terrors" are shared with others they lose their disabling power. Easter is a season of promise. There must have been moments of despair for early Christians which were met and conquered in Easter.

As the family gathers you may want to have a table setting of Halloween masks, difficult math books, perhaps some sports equipment. (The setting should reflect symbols which suggest fear.) The parents may want to act as facilitators during this time together. The mother or father can begin the activity by sharing some of the fears that were present as they faced parenthood. "I used to wake up at night and wonder if we would be able to take care of all the needs of a baby," one father remarked at a service like this. "I was afraid I'd drop you," the mother said to the oldest child. The sharing of little fears may help members of the family begin to see how frightening the unknown can be. When children are young, they sometimes frighten themselves in Halloween costumes but quickly learn that there is nothing harmful in the ugly face or weird dress. There are other fears, however, not so easily overcome. One young girl told her family at a gathering like this that her stomach hurt every day at school during geometry class. "I finally realized that I was never going to be able to learn geometry at all unless I did something about being scared."

Give each person a chance to share some experience of fear. Then provide the members of the family with copies of the "Litany of Faith." You may want to explain that the psalmist uses literary terms to describe some of the feelings persons have when they are filled with fear.

Ask the family members to divide, half of them reading the section on faith, the other half the section on fear.

Faith: Unto thee our fathers cried and were delivered; in thee they trusted, and were not put to shame.

Fear: A herd of bulls surrounds me, great bulls of Bashan beset me. Ravening and roaring lions open their mouths wide against me.

Faith: But do not remain so far away, Lord; O my help, hasten to my aid. Deliver my very self from the sword, my precious life from the axe.

Fear: My strength drains away like water and my bones are loose.

Faith: Praise him, you who fear the Lord; all you sons of Jacob, do him honor; stand in awe of him, all you sons of Israel.

Fear: My heart has turned to wax and melts within me. My mouth is dry and my tongue sticks to my jaw.

Faith: But God has not scorned the downtrodden, nor shrunk in loathing from his plight, nor hidden his face from him; God gave heed to him when he cried out.

Fear: I am laid low in the dust of death. The huntsmen are all about me; a band of ruffians rings me round.

Faith: Let those who seek the Lord praise him and be in good heart forever.

(Psalm 22)

Following this reading together, the group may respond to the following scripture read by a member of the family:

"God has not given us the spirit of fear; but of power and of love, and of a sound mind."—II Timothy 1:7.

The family members may affirm together:
"God give us the spirit of hope.
We are sent forth freed from the spirit of fear."

cɛlɛBRAtɛ, cɛlɛBRAtɛ

This activity may be most appropriately held at the end of the day. One of the parents may announce at breakfast that sometime during the day each person is to find a symbolic gift to share with every other member of the family. (This is to be something which only *symbolizes* a gift.) The objects do not necessarily have to be kept. For instance, one gift may be an old watch or a clock, and the giver may say, "I'm giving this to you to symbolize the time I want to spend with you in the future." Another symbolic gift is a pair of scissors. The person presenting them may say that they symbolize the fun times to be had in the future—"cutting up." All symbols are to be determined by the individuals. They can be humorous or serious.

At the end of the day, when the family members gather together, each person brings a symbolic gift for every other person in the family. The celebration begins with the reading of the following by Helen Pearson:

Voice 1: Today, the Lord steps into the air once more to taste its color and feel its songs. He inhales the thoughts of children, the breath of yesterday, the fantasies of tomorrow, and he wonders whether his children are too old to celebrate their dreams.

Voice 2: Today, spin him your dreams.
And celebrate, celebrate, celebrate!
Celebrate because someday soon people will

Voice 3: Celebrate life every day.

Voice 4: Send up balloons in church.

Voice 5: Turn tired old cathedrals into cafeterias.

Voice 6: Paint gravestones as bright as the sun.

Voice 1: Know they are beautiful—black, red, yellow, or white.

Voice 2: Glimpse the face of God in others.

Voice 3: Use the eyes of friends in place of mirrors.

Voice 4: Bounce through the mountains on beachballs.

Voice 5: Sink their teeth into politics for peace.

Voice 6: Have senses in their souls as sharp as radar.

Voice 1: Grow flowers in their garbage cans.

Voice 2: Turn all bombs into boomerangs.

Voice 3: And switchblades into tubes of finger paint.

Voice 4: Run through the White House with muddy feet.

Voice 5: Hang Christmas banners from the moon.

Voice 6: Cover their cars with foam rubber.

All: Become as free as that man called Jesus the Christ.

Following this reading, each person distributes his or her gifts, taking time to indicate what they symbolize. The parents may want to bring in a small empty box which they explain is a "wish box." During the week, each member of the family is to write on a slip of paper some wish for every other member of the family. The box will be placed somewhere in the house where it can serve as a reminder. The wishes will be shared at a later time, but they are to help the family members keep each other in mind. In one family when the wish box was opened there were four sheets of paper, with the word "love" written in a first grader's careful printing. The papers did not have the names of the recipient on them. As an explanation, the six-year-old said, "I just gave everyone a wish for love because I couldn't think of anything better to wish for."

Fruit juice should be provided for each person as part of the sending forth from this celebration. A special toast may be offered by one person on behalf of the entire family:

"Send us forth to celebrate.
Send us forth to rejoice.
Send us forth to live."
Cookies or donuts or some other special treat may be served following the sending forth.

OUR many selves

A helpful resource for this time together is the book *The Many Selves of Ann-Elizabeth* by Evelyn Maples. In a family where there are several adults, another helpful resource is *Our Many Selves* by Elizabeth O'Connor. (Both of these books may be ordered from Herald House.)

You may want to use the poem by Dietrich Bonhoeffer as a discussion starter with older youth and adults. As preparation for Easter a meaningful activity can help to affirm the unique selves represented in each individual. If the book about Ann-Elizabeth is used, you will have a natural introduction to the following experience:

Provide magazines and scissors for all in the group and ask them to cut out faces which describe some of the ways they have seen themselves. For instance, a child may cut out a face of someone who has an angry expression, another smiling, and another looking pleased. These show how the child has felt or acted. Paste these pictures on sheets of paper. Put them on the table and examine them to see how many expressions reflect joy, sadness, anger, pain, etc. Now you may want to share a part of a song from Mister Rogers:

> Myself, myself
> I'd like to be myself
> I'd like to let the people see
> the genuine inside of me
> Myself! Myself! I'd like to be myself.

Now ask the group to think about what it means to be "myself." After having shared the pictures of the different facial expressions and the story of Ann-Elizabeth, can a person say exactly what "myself" is every moment of the day? You may want to share this reading:

First Child: Sometimes I am an angry person [frowns] —I look like this.

Second Child: Sometimes I am a happy person [smiles] —I look like this.

Parent: Sometimes I am a tired person [looks tired] —I look like this.

Parent: Sometimes I am a thoughtful person [looks thoughtful] —I look like this.

First Child: But I am sometimes a happy person [smiles], tired [looks tired], and thoughtful person [looks thoughtful].

Second Child: So am I. And I am an angry person sometimes, too.

Parent: So am I.

Parent: So am I.

All: We are all many selves. We are not just one person all the time.

Second Child: And God loves us all the time.
First Child: Even when we are angry?
Second Child: Yes—and when we are tired or
　　　　thinking or angry.
Parent: God loves us all the time.
Parent: God loves us as we are.
All: God loves our many selves.
　　　　Thank you, Lord.

Who Am I?

Who am I? They often tell me
I stepped from my cell's confinement
calmly, cheerfully, firmly,
like a Squire from his country house.

Who am I? They often tell me
I used to speak to my wardens
freely and friendly and clearly,
as though it were mine to command.

Who am I? They also tell me
I bore the days of misfortune
equably, smilingly, proudly,
like one accustomed to win.

Am I then really that which other men tell of?
Or am I only what I myself know of myself?
Restless and longing and sick, like a bird in a cage,
struggling for breath, as though hands were compressing
　　　　my throat,
yearning for colours, for flowers, for the voices of birds,
thirsting for words of kindness, for neighbourliness,
tossing in expectation of great events,
powerlessly trembling for friends at an infinite distance,
weary and empty at praying, at thinking, at making,
faint, and ready to say farewell to it all.

Who am I? This or the other?
Am I one person to-day and to-morrow another?
Am I both at once? A hypocrite before others,
and before myself a contemptible woebegone weakling?
Or is something within me still like a beaten army
fleeing in disorder from victory already achieved?
Who am I? They mock me, these lonely questions of mine.
Whoever I am, Thou knowest, O God, I am thine!

—Dietrich Bonhoeffer,
The Cost of Discipleship,
the Macmillan Co., New York, N. Y.
1960

good friday

Good Friday—a time of sorrow and song—can be a
meaningful experience. Sometimes families mourn the
death of a neighbor as well as relatives. If the sense of
grief is inexpressible at the time of the death, the
Lenten season may prove an appropriate period to
remember the loss.

You may want to play the song, "Turn, Turn,
Turn," by Pete Seeger. (It has been recorded by a
number of popular artists, including Joan Baez and
Judy Collins.) This is based on the scripture in
Ecclesiastes 3:1-8:

To everything there is a season, and a time to every purpose
under heaven;
A time to be born, and a time to die; a time to plant, and a time
to pluck up that which is planted;

A time to kill, and a time to heal; a time to break down, and a time to build up;

A time to weep, and a time to laugh; a time to mourn, and a time to dance;

A time to cast away stones, and a time to gather stones together; a time to embrace, and a time to refrain from embracing;

A time to get, and a time to lose; a time to keep, and a time to cast away;

A time to rend, and a time to sew; a time to keep silence, and a time to speak;

A time to love, and a time to hate; a time of war, and a time of peace.

You may also be interested in the record "Seasons" by the Medical Mission Sisters which features another version of this scripture. (This may be ordered from Avante Guard Records, Inc., 250 West 57th Street, New York, New York, 10019.

The family is called together by a reading of the Scriptures or the suggested song.

A member of the family: There is a time to remember.

All of the family: We remember happy times. (At this point each member of the family shares a particular memory of the person who has died.)

A member of the family: There is a time to remember.

All the family: We remember sad times. (Out of his memory each person shares something of his grief.)

A member of the family: But while we remember sad and happy times we are reminded by death itself that God's promise is resurrection. What a joyful surprise! This is a mystery, and perhaps no one really can understand it. Yet somehow we sense that those who are so real in our memory are not simply and finally dead.

All of the family: So we sing in our sorrow. We sing a song of joy.

The family sings together Hymn No. 29 in *The Hymnal.*

A member of the family may want to read this prayer:

Prayer of sorrow and song

God, you have made us to love each other.
Sometimes we suffer separation through death, and we feel pain.
Sustain us in our sorrow. Let our song of joy express our love for you, for the person from whom we are separated, and for each other.
In the name of the risen Lord, Jesus, amen.

EASTER

EASTER

In many nations Easter is spoken of as "Pascha"—the Christian Passover. Easter and the days dependent on it developed much earlier in Christian tradition than Christmas and the associated celebrative days. The relationship of the Christian celebration of the risen Lord and the Jewish observance of the central event of the old covenant, the deliverance from Egypt, is not coincidental. The synoptic gospels clearly state that the Last Supper was a celebration of the Passover.

Easter, too, has origins in the ancient pagan rites. The word "Easter" is used much later than the Christian tradition began. It is the Old English adaptation of *Eastre*, the Teutonic goddess of spring and dawn. The early Christians adopted the existing folk spring festivals to their own commemoration. Where primitive people had celebrated spring and the return of new life to the earth, the Christians celebrated the new Life that had come into the world which shall never die.

While the celebration included the knowledge that "while we were in sin, Christ died for us," and reflected a new understanding of freedom, Easter also became the highlight of the entire year in the Christian tradition. In medieval documents Easter is often referred to as the beginning of a new year, especially in France, where this custom prevailed until 1563. Easter was for the early church the most important historic event.

Some beautiful customs developed in the earliest days of the church which might be interesting to consider. In the early centuries, the faithful embraced each other with the words *"Surrexit Dominus vere"* (Christ is truly risen), to which the answer was *"Deo gratias"* (Thanks be to God). In the Greek Church the greeting is *"Christos aneste"* (Christ is risen), and the answer, *"Alethos aneste"* (He is truly risen).

The Council at Nicea (325) prescribed that on Sundays and during Easter time all Christians should pray standing, never bending their knees, to indicate that they were risen with Christ. (When you stand for prayer at church, perhaps the phrase "We are risen with Christ," may enter your mind.

In the first centuries of the church the Easter vigil began on Saturday evening and continued through the night. Early Christians anticipated that the Lord would return for the Last Judgment during one of these vigils. Lights were hung throughout the church. In many places persons stood waiting for the sunrise. The sunrise services which mark Easter celebrations have their roots in this all-night observance. According to a legend popular in the Middle Ages the sun dances on Easter morning or makes three cheerful jumps at the moment of rising in honor of Christ's resurrection. In many countries people gathered on hillsides and watched for the sun; sometimes bands and choirs would perform. The early morning sunrise services which mark the Easter celebrations in the twentieth century have their origins in these celebrations.

Although many persons feel that the commercialization of Easter has weakened its power, some of the customs associated with the materialism began apart from any attempt to emphasize externals.

In the early church Easter was one of the few times during the year when Christians were baptized. They wore new garments of white linen at this time. It became a tradition among all the faithful to appear in new clothes on Easter Sunday, symbolizing the "new life" that the Lord through his resurrection bestowed on all believers. This was widely practiced during medieval times. There is an ancient Irish saying, "For Christmas, food and drink; for Easter, new clothes."

The origin of the Easter egg goes back before Christian history. Primitive people must have been startled to see a new and live creature emerge from what seemed an inanimate object. The egg became the symbol of spring. In Christian culture the egg symbolized the tomb out of which Christ emerged to the new life of his resurrection. Since the egg was one of those foods forbidden during the observance of Lent, it became appropriate to share it as a special Easter gift. Members of the household of faith in early times painted Easter eggs in bright colors and shared them as gifts. In Russia and among the Ukrainian and Polish people, families used to start their joyful Easter meals after the long Lenten fast with a blessed egg on Easter Sunday. Before sitting down to breakfast the father would distribute small pieces cut from an Easter egg to each member of the family and guests. This was eaten in silence before partaking of the Easter meal.

The Easter lily was introduced in Bermuda from Japan in the middle of the nineteenth century. In 1882 a florist named W. K. Harris brought it to the United States where it was soon called the Easter lily because it bloomed during this period. The scriptural references to the lily made this transference quite easy.

Any flower which your family appreciates particularly could become your floral symbol of Easter. One family uses hyacinths each Easter season as gifts to other members of the family. The fragrance is a gentle reminder of the love which surrounds them. In countries in the Southern Hemisphere some autumn flower might have bestowed on it particular meaning if it is used in conjunction with the special observance of Easter.

The celebration of this most joyful event in the life of the Christian can include whatever symbols or activities enrich the life of your family. Although a celebration of Easter cannot be imagined apart from the community of faith in which the gathered body confesses the risen Lord, there are ways in which the family can make Easter a significant celebration. There may be some ancient customs your family may wish to restore to meaning, such as the greeting, "He is risen" and the reply, "He is risen indeed." However, you may want to create some new traditions.

The fifty days following Easter Sunday are considered part of the Easter season.

EASTER: THE PROMISE OF LIFE

Leader: Let us remember Easter
Family: We sometimes forget what the Easter celebration is all about.
Leader: Let us remember Easter.

Story

Loren Eisley has given us a description of a person who lives in hope in his book *The Unexpected Universe.* On the beaches of Costabel the tide sweeps in with the rhythm of a heartbeat, leaving behind many forms of sea life. Tiny shells, seaweed, and starfish are deposited. Then there in the sand and sun of each day the sea life dies. Tourists go out early in the morning to collect shells and starfish to take home. They look like vultures swooping down on some half-alive creation. But look ahead! What is that man doing?

He bends down, picks up an object, and flings it out beyond the breaking surf. He is picking up half-dead starfish and throwing them out as far as he can in the hope that the offshore pull will be strong enough to keep them from being swept back onto shore. He will not simply watch the starfish struggle in the sand and die. He defies the course of natural events. He shows us how important life is.

God is our star-thrower. He sees us struggling in our

selfishness and pride. He loves us even as we fail to love him. He loves us when we are not lovable.

Easter is God's way of saying "I love you. You matter very much. You are important to me." We celebrate the risen Lord at Easter.

The proof of God's amazing love is this: that it was while *we were sinners* that Christ died for us. Moreoever if he did that for us while we were sinners, now that we are men justified by the shedding of his blood, what reason have we to fear the wrath of God. If, while we were his enemies, Christ reconciled us to God by dying for us, surely now that we are reconciled we may be perfectly certain of our salvation through his living in us.... We may hold our heads high in the light of God's love because of the reconciliation which Christ has made.

—Romans 5:5-11, Phillips translation.

The family shares the meaning of the star-thrower story by responding to the statement: "I remember one time when I felt as if nobody cared about me and someone in the family..."(each person shares a time when someone brought hope).

The sending forth:

Leader: Our Father, you have called us to life in this world.

Family: Help us to help each other be glad for this life.

Leader: Help us to be star-throwers.

Family: Help us to remember your love.

Leader: Help us to love each other and others.

Family: Each other and others. Amen.

nourished in love

Each member of the family is given a blank sheet of white paper. Crayons are placed in the center of the table to be shared by all.

Members of the family will be given time to draw pictures. It may be helpful to have one of the older children facilitate this session. The pictures are to represent the family gathered for a meal on an occasion which the person remembers as special. For instance, in one family a child recalled a stormy winter evening when the family ate hot soup and sandwiches and "we all felt real close to each other." The person is to draw the members of the family (stick figures are perfectly acceptable) in colors which might describe the way the person appeared to feel. In the incident mentioned, the child drew his older sister "blue" because the phone lines were down and she couldn't talk to her boyfriend that evening. He drew his father black because "that is the strongest color and Dad was so strong and shoveled the walk later." He drew his mother red: "She was smiling and laughing because we had a fire in the fireplace all night, and because her cheeks got all red when she helped shovel the walk." He drew himself orange because he "got to stay up until almost sunrise, and I was so happy all the time we were snowed in." As the members of the family listened to the young boy recall a special time in their life together they began to remember meals in which a special kind of joy was expressed.

Ample time should be allowed for each family member to share in the memory. When all the drawings have been shared, the family may want to participate in this brief liturgy.

Voice 1: We thank God for food and shelter.
Voice 2: We thank God for the nurture of our family.
All: We thank God for the nourishment of joyful
      memories.

(This may be an appropriate time for any of the members of the family who wish to offer prayers of gratitude.)
All: We are sent forth stronger for our having been
   together.

love within the family

This activity will give family members an opportunity to evaluate their personal relationships with others in the family circle. The group can be called together with a cutting from the Galatian letter:

Leader (may be any member of the family):
You, my friends, were called to be free...
only do not turn your freedom into license for
your lower nature, but be servants to one
another in love.

All: For the whole law can be summed up in a
single commandment:
"Love your neighbor as yourself."

The checklist here should be printed or duplicated so that each member of the family has one to use. It is very important that every person have an opportunity to be as honest as he or she can be in responding to the questionnaire. These may be shared aloud, or they may be used by individuals to see where they stand in relationship to others. The major purpose of the checklist is to help each family member develop greater sensitivity to the others.

Ample time should be allowed for checking the list. Then the members may be asked if they wish to share their personal evaluations. This may be an excellent time for affirming the love which can strengthen and support.

LOVE WITHIN THE FAMILY

Here is a checklist to help you develop an awareness of yourself in the family circle. Mark the number on the scale that indicates your judgment of how love operates in your family. For example, if you feel your family always fits the description on the right, circle number 8; if the description on the left fits your family well, circle number 1. If you feel your family life is somewhere in between, circle the number you feel is appropriate.

Every person in my family is loved and appreciated.	1 2 3 4 5 6 7 8	No one in my family loves me.
When someone in my family is hurting inside we all try to help.	1 2 3 4 5 6 7 8	When I am hurting inside no one in my family cares.
Every person in my family is a good friend to every other person.	1 2 3 4 5 6 7 8	I am not important to anyone in my family.
Everyone in my family has a few really good friends.	1 2 3 4 5 6 7 8	I have no friends outside my family.
It is easy for all the people in my family to feel how another member is feeling.	1 2 3 4 5 6 7 8	I can't understand why other people in my family get upset or angry or cry.
All the members of my family care about the feelings and thoughts of the others. We are all persons, not things.	1 2 3 4 5 6 7 8	My family thinks I exist only to be used or to serve others.
My family will listen to me and consider my ideas along with the others in making family decisions.	1 2 3 4 5 6 7 8	I have no voice in any decisions made in my family.
Everyone in my family tries to let the others know the way he is inside.	1 2 3 4 5 6 7 8	I never let anyone in my family know what I *really* think or feel.
My family helps me to become who I am, even if that is different from other family members.	1 2 3 4 5 6 7 8	My family has lots of rules that cramp me and keep me from being who I am.

—Anne Lee Kreml. Family Actualization Scale included in an unpublished thesis "Understanding Conflict in the Normal Family: An Educational Model for Family Actualization." Chicago Theological Seminary, June, 1970.

celebrating change

A helpful resource for the very young for this time together is the reading enclosed, "Fuzzy Wuzzy Caterpillar." Another helpful resource is the book *Hope for the Flowers*. If it is possible to enlist the help of members of the family prior to the worship activity, you may want to make construction paper caterpillars for each person. The butterflies can be made as part of the shared time, or they may be made in advance of the gathering. Time and interest may be a factor here. Butterflies can be made by gathering pieces of bright-colored wrapping tissue with pipe cleaners which can be twisted to make antennae. If the butterflies have been made earlier, decorate the room with them, hanging them by thread from convenient objects.

The butterfly is a Christian symbol and is often used in observing Easter and sometimes Christmas in some faiths. The symbol of new life suggested in the butterfly can be understood by very young children as well as adults.

If the family members can share the story *Hope for the Flowers*, there may be opportunity to discuss the risk taken when a person decides to change. In families with small children, the story may be shared for the simple joy of the story itself.

Following the story, you may want to participate in

the following: Have a member of the family read Romans 12:1-2 in your family's favorite Bible translation. Following this, share ideas about the symbolism of the butterfly. Some of these questions may be discussed: Is the caterpillar created to be "just a caterpillar"? What happens when it becomes a butterfly? What do the words "conform" and "transform" mean? How can the word "transform" be used in the description of the caterpillar and the butterfly?

After the discussion you may want to share the following reading:

Voice 1: If a person is in Christ

All: That person is new!

Voice 2: All things are changed.

All: That person is new!

Voice 3: Life takes on new meanings.

All: We are made new!

We are like butterflies from caterpillars—
new creatures.

Make us new, God.

FUZZY WUZZY CATERPILLAR

A fuzzy, wuzzy caterpillar wiggled up a tree.
    (One hand wiggles up the other arm)

He wiggled long, he wiggled short
    (Wiggle hand the entire length of arm, then just a
        short distance)

Then he wiggled right at me.
    (Jump back as if afraid)

I caught him and put him in a big glass jar and
  screwed the lid on tight
    (Pretend to catch between two hands, put down
    in jar, and screw on lid)

And said, "Now don't you go away. I'll be right back."
    (Shake finger toward pretend jar)

But when I got back there wasn't any caterpillar—
    (Shake head)

There was a butterfly instead,
    (Wave hands as if flying)

Now I can't make a butterfly even if I try.
    (Pretend to be trying to make something with
    hands)

Only God can make a butterfly.
    (Point to sky)

WE BEAR BURDENS OF OTHERS

Easter is a dramatic reminder of the love of God and an excellent time for the family to express appreciation for Christ who bore the burden of humanity's sin. An effective observance can be built around this theme by putting a large nail before the place of each person at the table. (The nail is a symbol of crucifixion.) Somebody in the family—probably one of the adults who plans the service—can begin by holding his or her nail up before the group and saying, "I have hurt someone this week." This is followed by a confession of what he or she has done. But, most important, after this is said the nail is passed to the person sitting beside the one who has confessed. This person then turns and says, "God has already forgiven you, you are loved. You are free." This person then keeps the nail, and the action is repeated by every other member of the family. The drama of confession and pardon is an experiential way of expressing the meaning of Easter.

The family may then read together:

All: Yet the proof of God's amazing love is this: that it was *while we were* sinners that Christ died for us. Moreover if he did that for us while we were sinners, now that we are men justified by the shedding of his blood, what reason have we to fear the wrath of God? If, while we were his enemies, Christ reconciled us to God by *dying for us*, surely now that we are reconciled we may be perfectly certain of our salvation through his *living in us.*—Romans 5:9.

A paraphrase of the scripture may have more meaning for a family in which there are young children—perhaps something like this:

All: The way God has shown us how much he loves us is that even when we are not lovable, he still loves us. We are accepted by God just as we are. We have been shown his great love in Christ. While what we do may not be okay, we are okay. This is why we can say to others who have hurt us, "You are already forgiven. God loves you."

This would be an excellent opportunity for the family to learn the hymn "Amazing Grace."

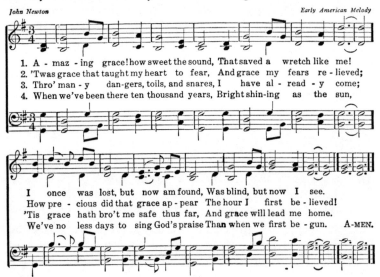

John Newton

Early American Melody

1. A - maz - ing grace! how sweet the sound, That saved a wretch like me!
2. 'Twas grace that taught my heart to fear, And grace my fears re - lieved;
3. Thro' man - y dan - gers, toils, and snares, I have al - read - y come;
4. When we've been there ten thousand years, Bright shin-ing as the sun,

I once was lost, but now am found, Was blind, but now I see.
How pre - cious did that grace ap - pear The hour I first be - lieved!
'Tis grace hath bro't me safe thus far, And grace will lead me home.
We've no less days to sing God's praise Than when we first be - gun. A-MEN.

WE CELEBRATE OUR HERITAGE

Some religious bodies observe days of celebration in which those who are dead are honored—such as the Catholic "All Saints' Day" and the Anglican "Doctors, Missionaries, and Martyrs Day." There is merit in remembering those who have passed on a heritage of faith.

Some families may wish to use April 6 to celebrate the establishment of the church. This would be the appropriate time also to recall special events in their own history involving church members whose service has enriched their lives. Statements such as the following may be made:

"I am grateful for the heritage that is mine because of the commitment of Joseph Smith. He was a person who sought new understandings about God. He was a man of faith."

or

"I am grateful for the heritage that is mine because of the faithfulness of Emma Smith. She was a courageous woman who served others and God."

or

119

"I am grateful for the devotion of Joseph Smith III who helped the Reorganized Church become a forward-looking institution. He encouraged people to work in their communities and brought a reconciling ministry to the Saints."

or

"I am grateful for the heritage that is mine because of Marietta Walker. She helped develop an awareness of the need for higher education. She also knew the value of the printed word."

or

"I am grateful for the heritage that is mine because of Paul M. Hanson. He served the church and his fellowman with a trust in God and an appreciation of the time in which he lived. He was not afraid of the future."

or

"I am grateful to the church because of the heritage that is mine because of the ministry of John J. Garver. He was a zestful disciple of the Lord Jesus who celebrated life."

or

"I am grateful for the heritage that is mine because of Fannie Pender Page. She was the first woman to go alone on a mission. In 1921 she went to the British West Indies for the church. She was a woman of skill and courage."

or

"I am grateful for the courage of Caroline Booker who began life as a slave. Her witness was to live as a free woman, even while in bondage. Her testimony of the power of restoration and the Spirit of God continues to strengthen persons."

These are statements about persons from the past. Family members may have memories of some stalwart of the faith whose life is a more recent part of their heritage. They may wish to share such memories with a statement beginning "I am grateful for the life of_____."

Another way to enhance this activity is to engage in tombstone rubbing. This is done preferably with rice paper, although shelf paper may be used. The paper is placed on the design of a marker, then rubbed with charcoal or a special "old Tombstone" crayon. This activity is one many children enjoy, particularly if the visit is to a historic cemetery. There is much to be discovered just by reading the headstones of graves. One church school class that visited a cemetery to do tombstone rubbings found the grave of a famous pioneer. Some of the young people in the class were unaware that he had been a citizen of their community. Frequently children gain a greater appreciation of how dear family members are to each other by reading the legends on tombstones and discovering how frequently very young children died in the 1700's and 1800's. This is an activity all members of the family can share and then come together to describe their feelings about the experience.

If the tombstone rubbing activity is chosen, the celebration of heritage may follow. It can be appropriately closed with each member of the family expressing gratitude to God for some specific gift he/she feels has come down through past generations to the present family.

the family explores the possibility of sharing

During a week there might be several ways in which the family can experience new dimensions of sharing. These moments need to be carefully thought through but not rigidly structured. The promise inherent in these times together may be realized at the spontaneity characterized in the Holy Spirit.

Perhaps the members of the family might come together to share feelings. At the places at the table, or wherever you may choose to gather, have a magic marking pen and a blank piece of white paper. Have each person take only a few moments to draw his or her feelings. (No words may be used.) This effort will be shared with other members who may try to describe how the person is feeling by using such words as happy, sad, lonely, tired, excited, restless, enthusiastic, etc.

After others have guessed what the person was "saying," he or she may then share the feeling expressed

in the drawing. This activity can help the family respect and appreciate the deep feeling each member has.

Occasionally a very simple meal of bread and water (or milk) may be served. The mealtime discussion might be directed toward hunger prevalent throughout the world. The family may want to contribute the money saved in that meal to an organization such as World Missions Health, UNICEF, CARE, or CROP.

At another time the family may want to discuss sharing time with others. There may be someone in the congregation or community who needs special attention. One family visited a local rest home and discovered three elderly people who had no relatives in the area. Each person determined when he or she could share an hour with one of these people. The friendships that developed continued. Sometimes a member of the family would discover opportunity to spend half a day with a person who had at one time felt that no one cared. Perhaps there may be relatives who are lonely also. This activity can be expanded to include the People-to-People program, American Field Service Students, or Big Brother Program. The sharing here is not only of time but—more important—of self.

Time is needed to develop a corporate, intentional life together. In many instances, unless some deliberate effort is made to share responsibility, the physical burden for a family will fall largely to the mother and father. Coming together to determine which tasks fit the skills and gifts of the various members can provide a rich opportunity to share. One family lists chores on sheets of paper and the members draw a number of tasks for the week. Another has an unwritten agreement that each member will be aware of the tasks that need to be done and if possible do them as he or she becomes aware. (This may break down without discussion, since awareness levels vary radically in family members. One thirteen-year-old boy walked through ankle-high grass without being aware that the back lawn needed mowing until he lost a baseball. The lawn was mowed the next morning.)

The family may have many resources to share with others. Money and time are not the only offerings which can be made. However, as the family develops in the stewardship of sharing, time and money may be invested in local political and social concerns, in needs of people who are strangers but are hungry or in pain, in enriching the cultural life of the family.

Undoubtedly there are many possibilities which are unique to your particular family. Watch for them.

trinity

trinity

Trinity is the longest season on the Christian calendar. It covers the period between Eastertide and Advent. In some traditions it is divided into several segments, including Pentecost or Whitsuntide, which is celebrated the fiftieth day after Easter and Kingdomtide. In many traditions Kingdomtide has been twelve weeks of the year when social concerns have been emphasized in the church.

As a season Trinity includes various opportunities for the family to develop new symbols of Christian life, new ways of expressing love and concern for those who are not part of the family. Trinity is an opportunity to respond to the message of Easter. The reality of a living Christ can enable the family to enrich its understanding of what it means to be covenanted to God and each other.

Some of the events that occur in Trinity which embrace summer and fall in the Northern Hemisphere are the ending of school, Children's Day, Father's Day, and the First Day of Summer; in the United States, Independence Day, Columbus Day, Halloween, and Thanksgiving. In other nations, such as Australia, holidays during this season include the Queen's Birthday and Labor Day. National holidays, special times in the family, the changing seasons, and events that have particular meaning to individuals in the family can be part of the celebration of the living God observed during Trinity.

WE ARE A missional family

The Easter season is over. For more than twenty weeks the family will be celebrating the season of Trinity. There are countless opportunities to make this a particularly meaningful experience. Perhaps Trinity can be introduced by a short liturgy in which family members accept the commission to share in redeeming and reconciling God's work. This they can do by sharing a covenant statement together. (The leader may be any member of the family.)

Leader: God has loved us into being. We do not exist for ourselves. We live in relationship with others. Let us affirm our life together at this point in history.

(The following covenant statement may be printed and given to each member of the family who will fill in the blanks. It may also be placed on a large blackboard or poster.

All: I am a member of the _____
(name your family)

family. I am a citizen of the universe,

of the world, of _____,
(name the hemisphere)

of_____, of the_____,
(name your nation)   (name the region of your nation)

of_____, of _____,
(name your state)   (name your town)

of_____.
(name your congregation)

Voice 1: All of these memberships help us know who we are and demand much from us. We are called to be the church in all these places where we find ourselves. God's concern extends to our family and to all persons in the universe. We are called to help share the love of God and to care for others.

Voice 2: As persons loved of God we come together now to declare that we are citizens in all these places, but we have chosen to serve God in a special way in the place where we are now.

Voice 3: Here in this place we agree to share the hurt of people, to listen to each other, and to speak of common concerns. We pledge ourselves as a unit bound together in love to lose ourselves in service to others.

Voice 4: We commit ourselves to reconciling, redeeming concerns.

All: Thus it is that we go forth in love and in peace. Amen.

this is our father's world

For the worship activities for the next four weeks the family might consider the needs of the earth. It may be helpful for some member to create a large montage on which the word "Ecology" is printed with the following definition: The Mutual Relationship of Creation. Pictures of ecological concerns may be pasted around the statement. If there are older children in the family, they may want to present the drama "Our Landlord Is a Softy."

Our Landlord Is a Softy

Scene: A pearly-lit executive suite. The Landlord, seated on a throne-like chair, is listening to the annual year-end report of his Chief Collection Agent, Mr. Gabriel.

Mr. Gabriel: And so, Sir, there's no question that you have a beautiful piece of property there, all right. Ah, the way the grass smells after a rain. The brilliance of a snowfield on a crisp morning. The softness of a desert in the moonlight. The way a sea fog creeps in—

The Landlord (sighing): Yes, yes, Gabriel, I know. But let's get down to the facts and figures. What about depreciation this past year?

Mr. Gabriel (shaking his head): Not so good, Sir. They've burned some more holes in Vietnam...and frayed the Arab-Israeli border rather badly.

129

The Landlord: Just write it off under "Normal Wear and Tear," Gabriel.

Mr. Gabriel (dubiously): Well, if you say so, Sir. But what about the air?

The Landlord: Well, what about the air?

Mr. Gabriel (consulting notes): They've poured another 16.2 million tons of exhaust fumes, industrial smoke and other garbage into the air, Sir. Really, it's rapidly lowering the value of the entire property. (grudgingly) Of course, I will say they didn't make it as radioactive as they did the year before.

The Landlord (nodding): See? That's an encouraging note.

Mr. Gabriel: But it's a different story with the water supply.

The Landlord (sadly): I suppose it is.

Mr. Gabriel: Yes, they've dumped 13.2 trillion more gallons of sewage, mud, industrial chemicals and other poisons into virtually every rivulet, creek and river. You cannot lie on your belly and drink from a cool, clear stream any more without chancing typhus, hepatitis, cholera....

The Landlord (holding up his hand): Please, how were crops? I assume they've been growing things.

Mr. Gabriel: Yes. I was going to get to soil erosion next. During the past 12 months no less than 82.5 billion tons of rich loam...

The Landlord (hastily): But they have been improving the property, I'm sure. What about new construction?

Mr. Gabriel: Yes. Let's see, they have built 112,232 new public buildings, all of which they claim will look very nice. Once the trees grow. They have also erected 27,342 new oil derricks on once-pleasant hillsides, paved over 43 alpine meadows with freeways and...

The Landlord (wincing): Not the alpine meadows!

Mr. Gabriel (relentlessly): Yes, the alpine meadows. And thanks to advances in rocketry, they reached new heights with their debris. While, at the same time, they have been busy drilling a deep hole into the earth. To see what's inside.

The Landlord: It's more curiosity than vandalism.

Mr. Gabriel: Sir, you must face facts. You have a beautiful piece of property and undesirable tenants. By any conceivable rule of property management, you have but one choice. (raising a golden horn to his lips) Shall I sound the eviction notice now?

130

The Landlord (hesitating): No. Let's extend their short-term lease for just one more year, Gabriel.

Mr. Gabriel: But you've been saying that for ages, Sir.

The Landlord (sighing deeply): I know, Gabriel. But I keep thinking that sooner or later they're going to stop acting as though they owned the place.*

This may stimulate discussion about our treatment of God's world. You may want to sing the hymn "This Is My Father's World." Can your family write another stanza to this song in which you express concern about God's world and the need to care for it?

Here are some scriptures which may add meaning to a discussion if you choose not to use the drama:

The earth lies polluted under its inhabitants; for they have transgressed the laws, violated the statutes, broken the everlasting covenant.—Isaiah 24:5.

For with the judgment you pronounce you will be judged.—Matthew 7:2.

And I brought you into a plentiful land to enjoy its fruits and its good things. But when you came in you defiled my land and made my heritage an abomination.—Jeremiah 2:7.

What are some results of violating the land? Perhaps members of the family could cite ways they see a misuse of the earth in their own community. One specific way that has affected the entire world is evidenced in the energy shortages. Human beings are finally becoming concerned about the use of natural resources. After the family has discussed the preceding scriptures, the following poem may be shared:

---

*Arthur Hoppe, "Our Landlord Is a Softy," *San Francisco Chronicle*, December 29, 1964. Copyright 1964 Chronicle Publishing Company.

No Shortage

Voice 1:   An energy crisis?
Oh, yes, I suppose...
But children,
Only of one small type.

Voice 2:   There is still the
Energy of people
(Most powerful of all)
Strengthened by God's love,
Sped on by gratitude.

Voice 3:   Look, oh please, look!
Is there a shortage of sunrises
To lift the heart with freshness
   and with zest
Filled with dreams and hopes
Of a new day?

Voice 4:   Is there the threat of
Rationing of sunsets
Which blaze the energy of God's
   creation
In neon affirmation
Across the limitless ceiling
For a day-tired soul?

All: If there is a lack of anything
Anywhere in the universe
It is most sadly evident
In the shortness of
Man's spirit-sight....

—Billi Jo Carroll

Voice 1: Father, we acknowledge that we are more concerned about our wants than the world's needs.

Voice 2: We are aware that you love us even while we are selfish and greedy.

Voice 1: Help us to behave as people who are loved.

Voice 3: Help us to be caring and grateful.

Voice 4: Help us to be conscious and conscientious.

All: Send us forth with new spirit-sight. Send us forth to see your creation with new eyes, to hear with new ears, and to sing a new song of gratitude. Amen.

This Is My Father's World

Maltbie D. Babcock

Franklin L. Sheppard

1. This is my Fa-ther's world, And to my lis-tening ears,
2. This is my Fa-ther's world, The birds their car-ols raise,
3. This is my Fa-ther's world, O let me ne'er for - get

All na-ture sings, and round me rings The mu - sic of the spheres,
The morn-ing light, the lil - y white De - clare their Mak-er's praise.
That though the wrong seems oft so strong, God is the Rul-er yet.

This is my Fa-ther's world: I rest me in the thought
This is my Fa-ther's world: He shines in all that's fair;
This is my Fa-ther's world: The bat - tle is not done;

Of rocks and trees, of skies and seas; His hand the won - ders wrought.
In the rus-tling grass I hear him pass, He speaks to me ev-ery-where.
Je - sus who died shall be sat - is - fied, And earth and heaven be one.

—From *The Hymnal for Youth,* copyright 1950. Used with permission.

134

plant a tree

Arbor Day is a festival unique to the United States, but the purpose transcends national boundaries. The initial plan for celebration included devoting a day each year to the public planting of trees. Its scope extended, and today in some areas of the United States Arbor Day is an occasion for emphasizing the importance of forestry and for planting seedling trees to reforest waste lands. The spirit of Arbor Day can be celebrated any time a tree is planted.

Spring is an excellent time for the family to celebrate together the beauty of trees. Fall is also suitable for tree planting. In the modern world when air pollution and destruction of land by highways are ever present concerns, a meaningful experience can be developed around the planting of a tree.

As a family you will need to determine what kind of tree you wish to plant. (The budget will be a factor in determining this. Sometimes it is possible to obtain free trees through farmers, the local forestry association, or park service. Some trees are not expensive; others are quite expensive.) Having decided on the kind of tree, you will need to determine where you wish to plant the tree. If you are giving the tree to the community you will want to check with the local park department or whatever community agency is responsible for the area where you wish to place the tree.

Once the tree has been purchased you may wish to gather the family outside around the tree for a brief ceremony before it is planted.

Voice 1: To be a friend to the earth is to care for all living things.
Voice 2: We celebrate life by planting a tree.
Voice 1: Trees provide a place for creatures to live.
Voice 2: Trees produce oxygen for us to use.

Voice 1: Trees add beauty with their fragrance, shape, and color.
Voice 2: Tiny hairs on the roots of trees hold the soil.
Voice 1: Trees absorb noise.
Voice 2: Trees enrich the ground with their fallen leaves.
Voice 1: Trees provide shade in which we can cool ourselves.
Voice 2: Trees absorb poisons from the air.
All: The tree is our promise of hope to those who come after us.

A prayer of gratitude is offered for trees.

All: We are sent forth to celebrate life.

The family sings together "Praise God from Whom All Blessings Flow."

to care for the earth

Before the family gathers one person may want to draw the following illustration on a chart:

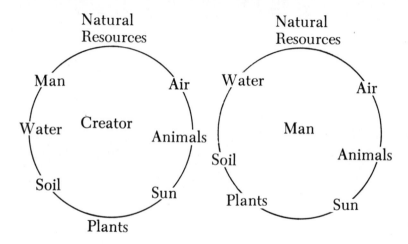

After all the members are together they may discuss the two charts, considering which model reflects their particular life-style. It may help to have one person read this modern version of Psalm 8:

> Lord, our Lord,
>   your greatness is seen in all the world.
> When I look at the sky, which you have
>   made,

at the moon and the stars, which you set
in their places—
What is man, that you think of him;
mere man, that you care for him?
Yet you have made him inferior only to
yourself;
you crowned him with glory and honor.
You made him ruler over all you have
made;
you placed him over all things:
sheep and cattle, and wild animals too:
the birds and the fish
and all creatures in the seas.
Lord, our Lord,
your greatness is seen in all the world!

—From *Good News for Modern Man*,
The New Testament and Psalms in
Today's English Version.
Copyright American Bible Society,
1966, 1971.

After listening to the Psalm together, each individual may share three ways in which he or she can develop better relationships with all of creation.

For a sending forth, the hymn "Lord of the Bronze-Green Prairies" in the *Supplement to the Hymnal* or "This Is My Father's World" may be used.

WE PLAN A CARING PROGRAM

The family is gathered with music (if possible). There are many contemporary songs that deal with ecological problems (e.g. Cat Steven's "Where Will the Children Play?," Joni Mitchell's "The Big Yellow Taxi," and Judy Collins' "Whose Garden Was This?").

A song which will introduce the idea may be helpful. The following statement may be read by a member of the family:

Many people these days wonder what it is like to be on a spaceship. They don't realize that they *are* on a spaceship all this time. It is a tiny little spaceship, only 8,000 miles in diameter. It is also a fantastically lonely little spaceship. The nearest star is 92 million miles away, and the next nearest star is so remote that it takes two and one-half years for its light to come to us. And yet this tiny spaceship is so superbly designed that it provides everything man needs for his journey through space. —R. Buckminster Fuller

The past few times worship has taken place, members of the family have tried to see ways in which they could more adequately care for the earth. Today their object will be to offer a specific time line of tasks which can be an offering of stewardship to God, on whose earth they are permitted to live.

It may be fun to pretend that the family is on a spaceship, and each person is to be responsible for certain tasks to keep the ship operating efficiently. Another member of the family may read the following:

140

Air pollution is caused by people. From the time we get up in the morning until we go to bed at night most of the things we use cause or have caused air pollution. We get up in the morning and turn on the light; much of our electricity is generated by burning fuels, and burning causes air pollution. We take a hot shower in water heated by burning gas. Our breakfast is cooked on a stove which uses fuel. The food itself gives off particles and gases into the air, as the fan on the kitchen vent will attest. The food may well have come from land which had been cleared by burning. We get into our car and drive to work; the automobile accounts for over half of our air pollution.

And if the things we use don't contribute directly to air pollution the chances are good that somewhere in their manufacturing process they were smelted, heated, abraded, ground, polished, sanded, or welded, etc., all of which contribute to air pollution. And when we are finished with the object and throw it out, it will probably be burned.—Bay Area Air Pollution Control District, "Air Pollution and the San Francisco Bay Area," San Francisco, 1969, p. 2.

Each member of the family may be asked to decide what tasks must be done to keep the spaceship Earth in orbit and a clean place to live. Then, on a large sheet of poster paper, a time line such as this may be drawn:

First week - Tasks	Persons responsible
First month - Tasks	Persons responsible
First year - Tasks	Persons responsible

What tasks are immediate, and who will take the responsibility for seeing that they are accomplished?

Here is a sample program of responsibility designed by one family:

First week

    Collect papers—Debbie

    Collect cans—Steve

    Collect bottles—Jon

(The children agreed to see that all materials which could be recycled were collected, cleaned, and stored for recycling at the end of the month.)

Plan menus to use food from garden—Dad
Check on use of lights and other fuel—Mom
(The family agreed that these tasks could be exchanged in coming weeks.)

First month

Write letters to government officials on ecology bills being considered.

Read aloud from the book *Ecology, A How and Why Wonder Book* (by Shelly and Mary Louise Grossman, Gosset and Dunlap, Inc., 1971) and/or *Everyman's Guide to Ecological Living* (by Greg Cailliet, Paulette Setzer, Milton S. Love, the Macmillan Co., 1971).

Take materials to recycling center.

If possible begin planning for a garden when the next planting season arrives.

First year

Learn to use the bike instead of the car whenever possible.

Cut down on the consumption of goods. Make things last, recycle materials. Rather than buying unnecessary gadgets for the yard and home, invest in trees, shrubs, and living plants. Over the year develop the life-style of caring.

After the family develops its own goals and time line

for achieving these, it may be appropriate to read the following scripture in unison:

These are portentous times. The lives of many are being sacrificed unnecessarily to the gods of war, greed, and avarice. The land is being desecrated by the thoughtless waste of vital resources. You must obey my commandments and be in the forefront of those who would mediate this needless destruction while there is yet day.

ÐECISIONS, ÐECISIONS, ÐECISIONS

The Christian family needs to be an intentional family. It has been said that "not to decide is to decide." The gathering today will use Doctrine and Covenants 58:6c-d as the basis for the activity.

Behold, it is not meet that I should command in all things, for he that is compelled in all things, the same is a slothful and not a wise servant; wherefore he receiveth no reward. Verily I say, Men should be anxiously engaged in a good cause, and do many things of their own free will, and bring to pass much righteousness; for the power is in them, wherein they are agents unto themselves.

This scripture may be put on a large sheet of paper, or the members of the family may want to use individual copies of the Doctrine and Covenants and a blank sheet of paper on which to write. The scripture may be copied at the top of a page of paper with space at the bottom for the exercise which follows:

Those who can do so may rewrite the scripture in their own words. If there are very young children in the family, perhaps the parents or one of the older children can help them decide what the scripture says to them.

Here is an example of the way an eight-year-old girl rewrote the scripture:

God doesn't want to have to tell me everything I am supposed to do, so he gave me a brain to think of things on my own. Everybody ought to be helping everyone else, because helping is the best way to live together. God expects me to help others.

A ten-year-old boy rewrote the scripture in this manner:

God doesn't want me to be lazy. He gave me agency and expects me to use it to do good. He doesn't want me to wait for him to have to tell me everything.

The purpose of this exercise is to help the members of the family find meaning in the scripture. Some of the difficulties persons have with scripture is that they are not able to get beyond the style of language to the deeper concepts.

Before the exercise you may want to discuss some of the language in order to help the children find the meaning. "It is not meet" is not a common expression. "Men should be anxiously engaged in a good cause" is a generic way of describing all persons. For the purpose of this exercise encourage people to write their versions in first person: "What does this scripture say to me?"

You may want to sing together a song from the junior high church school material "Freedom to Be." The song is sung to the tune of "Hi, Ho, Anybody Home" or "The Beachcomber's Song."

Free, free, free to decide
What this world is going to be;
This imperative is ours
To be free, free. . .(repeat)

You may enjoy singing this as a round.

Activities in the following weeks will be built on this experience.

Last week the family members struggled to rewrite in their own language Section 58:6 c and d. With this background, they may be ready to set some goals which can be realized by the entire group. Gathered around a table on which pencils and paper are available, they may want to participate in the following activity:

Have each family member think of two or three decisions made during the week. Try to determine how the decisions were made. Did the person analyze all the possibilities? Was there a specific reason for the choice that was made? Were the decisions made alone or with the help of others? Did the decision just "sort of happen"? Have each person share one of the decisions with the group.

Now have each person share with the group a decision that he or she is facing. What kinds of priorities have to be established? For instance, in one family the daughter was faced with the decision as to whether she would attend a swimming meet (the team needed her desperately), go to the state fair with her family (she had not been able to be with the family for some time), attend a League retreat (which she wanted to attend and felt would be worthwhile), or work at the local store where she had opportunity to do part-time work (she was saving money for music camp in the summer). No one tried to tell her what she *must* do. The family helped her list her concerns and the other persons who would be affected by her decision, then offered her love and support in her decision.

Each person needs to be free to make the final decision, but the family can be supportive by listening and helping the person see alternatives.

At the conclusion of this time together they may want to sing "Free to Decide" again.

MORE DECISIONS, DECISIONS

This is another opportunity to develop a greater sense of intentionality. Provide sheets of paper and pencils for each family member. Have all of them draw on a sheet of paper a diagram resembling a ladder. This should be large enough to fill the entire sheet. Draw in about five rungs (you may want more or less), then have each member write on each rung a priority (something that person feels the family should be doing). The top rung will represent the highest priority. When each person has finished, share the "ladders." Are they similar? Different? How do the individual members feel about the results? When these have been shared, use another sheet of paper on which another ladder has been drawn. Discuss ways in which you can determine which of these priorities every member can agree to, and then intentionally construct the ladder so that the priorities are clearly before the family.

One of the benefits of this time together may be to help members of the family see that each person views the group's needs through different eyes. This activity can be particularly helpful when a family is planning the budget or a vacation. The needs and perspective of each member are usually different. This exercise can help the family grow in its sense of corporate mission.

Following this exercise, you may want to stand in a circle, hold hands, and give each person an opportunity to commit himself or herself to achieving the first priority. This exercise can be repeated as goals are accomplished.

the family as individuals in community

Frequently the rush of each day keeps the family members from sensing a sustaining relationship to one another. Try to plan an evening when there can be flexibility in the time together. After all have gathered invite them to stand in a circle an arm's length apart. Invite each person to look at every other person in the circle—slowly and carefully. (There may be some giggling by younger children, but that should be accepted. People feel uncomfortable sometimes when they realize how seldom they honestly look at one another.) At this point you may want to say something like the following:

"Relax now and close your eyes. Look inward at yourself. Can you determine how you really feel? Are you happy? Are there problems that keep you from seeing yourself? Are you frustrated? Sad? Do you feel silly standing here with your eyes closed? Try not to think of anything but your own feelings. Can you think of things about yourself that no one else knows? Can you accept those things about yourself known only to you? What you are seeing now is you. No one else knows you as well as you know yourself.

"Bring your hands up before your face, keeping your eyes closed. Now, *open* your eyes and look at your hands. Look only at *your* hands—no one else's. Are your hands soft? Look at each individual finger. No one else in the world has a fingerprint like yours. No one in the world has ever had hands exactly like yours.

"Now try to think of what your hands have done. Do you use your hands a great deal? Have you sometimes used them in ways that were not helpful? Have you offered them to others who are in need? Your hands can symbolize you.

"Now reach out and take the hand of the person on each side of you. Close your eyes again. Try to see each person's face in your mind. Can you think of times your hands have hurt—or helped—these members of your family? Hold their hands tightly. As you stand clasping hands think of all the power, all the energy of those in the circle.

"Now, open your eyes and look into the face of the person on your right. Tell that person some way in which you want your hands to serve him/her. Do the same for the person on your left."

At this point, provide opportunity for persons to offer prayers on behalf of the family. Simple sentence prayers can be effective. A circular response in which each member of the family offers a brief prayer may be suggested.

A closing prayer, requested prior to this gathering, may then be offered. This prayer may include something of the following:

"God, we thank you that we have been so wondrously made. We thank you for the uniqueness we have sensed in ourselves. Forgive us when we have hurt others. Help us to use our hands to heal, not hurt; build, not destroy; reach out, not hold fast. Send us from our community into the world to be hands of friendship, service, and love. Amen."

welcome to summer

The family can celebrate at an outdoor breakfast in a park or an evening barbecue in the backyard. (This should be held on a beautiful day, of course.) Some of the music for this can be recorded on cassette and used at appropriate times in the celebration. (Suggested songs are "Here Comes the Sun," "Both Sides Now," "Summertime.")

After all have eaten together, they lie down, heads touching, so that each person is looking up at the sky. The song, "Both Sides Now" may be played while they watch clouds. Each can share what he or she sees in the clouds. (Young children usually find this delightful.)

After the cloud pictures have been shared, all may sit up and look straight ahead. Now the mother or father asks questions such as "What color do you see in the largest amount?" [The children may answer "green" for the grass, or there may be another color that dominates—perhaps "blue" for water or sky.] "How does the sun feel on your arms or legs or back?" [If the day is warm, the answers may be comments about how hot it is. The age of air conditioning brings greater awareness of the temperature of summer. "Here Comes the Sun" may be played now.]

Members of the family are given time to think of five reasons for being grateful for summer. After the reasons have been shared, Psalm 19 may be read.

A closing prayer can begin by saying, "Thanks, God, for summer." This statement may be followed by clapping or cheering. Then each person may thank God for a specific gift of summer, and after every statement the family can respond.

a secret friend

Summer is an excellent time to have a secret friend project. Usually the days are full of activity, but at other times they go by very slowly. In a family with young children, where older brothers and sisters have been in school all winter, summer is filled with excitement. It also should bring different responsibilities for each family member.

Several songs popular in recent years might be effective as gathering songs for the family in which there are teen-agers. Simon and Garfunkel's "Bridge Over Troubled Water," Carole King's "You've Got a Friend," or Judy Collins' "Pack Up Your Troubles" might be considered. Other favorites may also suggest the supportive relationship of a friend.

Write the name of each member of the family on individual slips of paper. When the group has gathered you may want to read together the following:

All: Oh, the comfort, the inexpressible comfort of feeling safe with a person, having neither to weigh thoughts nor measure words, but pouring them all right out, just

151

as they are, chaff and grain together; certain that a faithful hand will take and sift them, keep what is worth keeping, and then with a breath of kindness blow the rest away.

— Dinah Maria Mulok Craik

It may be beneficial to share in the singing of "Love Them Now" (introduced at an earlier time) found on pages 78 and 79. After the song has been sung, give the members of the family opportunity to draw names. The purpose of having a secret friend is to give each person unique support and encouragement. Gifts of kindness and thoughtfulness, done in secret on behalf of the person whose name has been drawn, will enhance the family spirit. The time of revealing secret friends can be established for several months later.

The following liturgy may be used to send the family forth.

All: Behold, how good and how pleasant it is. . .to dwell together in unity! (Psalm 133:1)

Voice 1: We are not only related to each other through our family, but we are related in love.

Voice 2: We are friends.

All: Behold, how good and how pleasant it is. . .to dwell together in unity!

Voice 3: I have a name in my hand. It is a special person.

Voice 4: I will be a special friend to my secret friend.

All: Behold, how good and pleasant it is. . .to dwell together in unity!

Voice 1: May we be sensitive to each other.

Voice 2: May we be thoughtful in our actions.

Voice 3: May we truly be friends.

152

All: Behold, how good and how pleasant it is. . .
to dwell together in unity! Make it so,
Lord. Amen.

This same liturgy may be used later at the time the
secret friends are revealed.

WE AFFIRM OUR FAITH

This celebration should be shared by all. You may
want to purchase paperback copies of the American
Bible Society New Testament *Good News for Modern
Man.* Each member of the family could have a
Testament to mark and use in this service and on other
occasions. The hymn of faith found in Philippians

2:1-11 can deepen an understanding of the coming season of Easter and enhance the celebration of the risen Lord.

This activity may take place around a table, outdoors, or in any setting where persons have light by which to read. If there are younger children in the family, you may want to help them memorize one of the shorter phrases in order to participate in the worship. The leader may very well be one of the children who has mastered reading and for whom this could be a welcome opportunity to share a skill. The leader's reading may need to be practiced; other parts may or may not need to be. (The first statement by the reader is paraphrased. The remainder of the reading is found in *Good News for Modern Man*.)

Leader: Does our life in Christ make us strong? with his Spirit? Do we feel kindness and compassion for one another? Let us share his love and grow in our unity together. Let us do away with selfish ambition or a desire to boast and learn to be humble toward each other. But let us look out for those beyond our circle as well as for one another. Let our attitude be a reflection of Christ's love:

Leader: He always had the very nature of God.

Voice 1: But he did not think that by force he should try to become equal with God.

Leader: Instead, of his own free will he gave it all up

Voice 2: And took the nature of a servant.

Leader: He became like man, he appeared in human likeness;

Voice 3: He was humble and walked the path of obedience to death—his death on the cross.

Leader: For this reason God raised him to the highest place above,

Voice 4: And gave him the name that is greater than any other name,

Leader: So that in honor of the name of Jesus,
All beings in heaven and on the earth,
and in the world below
Will fall on their knees,

All: And all will openly proclaim that Jesus Christ is the Lord,
To the glory of God the Father.

Leader: Let our praise to God be in our living.

All: Send us forth, Father, to live as servants in the name of Christ. Amen.

"according to our gifts"

A service in which we call from one another
the unique giftedness which is ours.

The leader in this service may be one of the parents or one of the children. Preparation should be made by all members of the family. Each person is to bring to the table something he or she enjoys doing. It may be a game, hobby, or something creative. These are to be placed on the table as the family gathers.

Leader: We have been called out to love one another. How shall we do this?

All: We listen for the signs and hints in others' lives in the very same way we listen for them in our own.

Leader: But sometimes we do not feel loved, creative, gifted.

All: The word of God to us in Christ is that we are loved, creative, gifted. Let us share this affirmation.

Each member of the family shares the symbol of his or her giftedness. Following this time of sharing symbols, the family responds in this manner:

Father to Mother (taking her hands in his): I thank God for the giftedness of you.

Mother to child beside her (taking the child's hands in hers): I thank God for the giftedness of you.

This continues from one member of the family to another.

Leader: The Scriptures tell us that all are called according to the gifts of God unto them. We have been called. We are now sent forth to express our unique gifts to others. Amen.

All: Amen.

the "you-ness" of others

This particular liturgy is designed to help members of the family see each other in a new way. The ideal setting is around the family dinner table on which candles are being used. One of the parents can begin by getting up from the table and addressing one of the children with whom she or he may have had trouble relating. Turning the light switch on and then off again, the parent may say something like this: "_____, sometimes when we are having a misunderstanding, I realize that I do not listen to you as I should. I think perhaps I treat you about like the light switch. I just turn you on or off. I want to treat you as a person, not as an object. I want to affirm now the 'you-ness' of you."

The parent then sits down at the table, takes a teaspoon, and holds it up to the candlelight so that the child who is being addressed can see his or her reflection. The parent says: "Can you see how the image of your face appears in the spoon? Sometimes I see your image in a distorted way. But tonight I see you as a person who has a unique quality." (The parent then tells the child one of his or her strengths. Perhaps the child is particularly truthful or quiet. The purpose of this moment is to mention something that will help the person feel unique and accepted.)

Following this, the parent asks the person sitting on the right to speak to the member of the family in the next place, using a spoon and affirming the strength of that person. When each person has been affirmed the family may wish to share the following:

Mother: God, you have brought us to this moment in our life together.

Father: Often we fail to see or hear or touch each other as persons.

Child 1: Instead we treat one another indifferently.

All: Forgive us, God.

Child 2: But you accept and love us in separation from each other and you.

Child 3: You call us, by your Spirit, to see each other as individuals.

All: Thank you, God.

Mother: Now we see ourselves and each other without distortion.

Father: We see our family in a new relationship.

Child 4: We see ourselves as able to be for one another and others.

All: Send us forth to be your people, God.

BE AS A CHILD

There are many persons today who feel that the freedom and imagination of children are qualities which are frequently denied by adults. These qualities offer opportunities to experience joy and exhilaration. Perhaps this play experience will create a spontaneous celebration.

Have the family members stand in a circle, holding hands. Now imagine that someone has tossed a ball in the circle. One person is to reach out, catch the imaginary ball, and toss it to someone else. After a few minutes of this activity ask one member of the family to place the imaginary ball in the center of the circle. Then all move to the center, and each person places a hand on the top of the imaginary ball at the same time. (The hand of each person will touch another hand.) Then join hands and walk around the imaginary ball. Each person is to describe the ball as he/she sees it.

After this exercise in imagination, you may want to sit down on the floor and give each person an opportunity to do something to make the others laugh. This "childhood game" can be demanding for adults because it requires a willingness to "be a child."

After sharing together in a time of laughter, provide opportunity for responses to the statement, "I remember when I was very young, the funniest thing happened...." This time of sharing memories can draw a family close together.

You may want to use the following to send the family forth:

Voice 1: God, we hear you in the sound of laughter.

Voice 2: We see you in joyful faces.

Voice 3: We sense you in the midst of our family life together.

All: For this we give thanks.

Voice 1: You have given us the gift of imagination.

Voice 2: You have given us the ability to laugh.

Voice 3: You have given us the power to love.

All: For this we give thanks.

Voice 1: You have made us a family.

Voice 2: You have called us to love each other and others.

Voice 3: You have blessed us with your love.

All: For this we give thanks.

Voice 1: Teach us to share our joy with others.

Voice 2: Lead us to those with whom we can share our gifts.

Voice 3: Send us to places where love is needed.

All: Send us forth, O Lord. Amen.

mαδε ιη τhε ιmαGε οf GOδ

For one week members of the family will have an opportunity to experiment with the effects of television advertising on their thinking. During this time they hopefully will be intentional in their TV viewing. Stan Freberg, who writes many of the humorous prize-winning commercials, suggests a week like this:

Monday: Television as usual.
Tuesday: The set goes black, but one word shines in the center of the screen: "Read!"
Wednesday: Television as usual.
Thursday: The set goes black again, but this time we see the word "Talk!"
Friday: Television as usual.
Saturday: The words "Unsupervised Activity" appear.

Sunday: Twenty-four glorious, uninterrupted hours of advertising.*

If television station managers were to take this clever schedule seriously, there might be an increase in church attendance. Some advertising is annoying, some is in poor taste, and much is inane. But the media informs, and advertising may frequently project an image by which viewers judge ourselves. For instance, do you find yourself influenced by emphasis on certain products? Do members of the family know the words to many of the commercials? For one week try the following project:

Choose some themes that recur in advertising such as "the best is..." "happiness is...," "for lasting value...," "to be loved...," "for quality...." As a family try to work out some definitions of the words above:

> Happiness is
> The best means
> Lasting value is
> Quality is
> To be loved is

Now with the definitions agreed upon, watch the advertisements for an entire week. Note how many of these agree with and how many are contradictory to the definitions arrived at by the family.

You may want to discuss the kinds of images of persons portrayed in the ads. What is a father like in most of the ads? What is a mother like? How are men pictured? How are women shown? What sort of

*From *Discovery in Advertising*, Paulist Press.

picture of children do the ads attempt to show? What are boys like? What kind of image of girls was shown? Are these images true to the images the individuals in the family have of themselves? of others?

Following your discussion at the end of the week you may wish to find some of the commercials in magazines that use expressions you have discussed. Make a poster of these slogans and place this scripture in the center:

> Don't let the world around you squeeze you into its mold, but let God remold your minds from within, so that you may prove in practice that the plan of God for you is good, meets all his demands and moves toward the goal of true maturity.
> —Romans 12:2 (Phillips).

Hang the poster in an appropriate place where individuals may view it often.

As a sending forth, you may wish to use the following:

Voice 1: Every day we are bombarded with images.

Voice 2: We question our own worth:

> Are we pretty or handsome enough?
> Do people like us?
> Do we impress others?

Voice 3: Help us, God, to allow your Spirit to work in our lives.

Voice 4: Help us see ourselves as loved and accepted by you.

All: Don't let the world squeeze us into its own mold.

> Remold us in your image, God.
> And send us forth to be your people.

special day celebrations

Several celebrations will follow which will be planned around special occasions in the family. A suggested symbol of these occasions is a robe that each member of the family wears during the worship and celebration. This should be inexpensive and creative, not elaborate. Unbleached muslin or old sheets can be decorated with magic markers, fabric paints, or appliques made of scraps. The pattern suggested is a simple "sack-like" costume with an opening for the head and arms.

This will be donned on special days in the lives of family members, such as birthdays. Perhaps the different members of the family can plan a celebration which is in keeping with the interests and personality of the birthday person. Gifts for the occasion can be creative and not necessarily expensive. In one family where the junior-high daughter was just developing an interest in art, each member of the family gave her some item to build up her store of art supplies. But beyond that, one of her brothers, who was old enough to drive the car, gave her a ticket that said, "This entitles you to two trips to the art museum—transportation provided." The younger sister gave her a ticket that said, "This guarantees that your chores will be done for you when you make the two trips to the museum." Her parents made arrangements with an artist friend for her to visit the studio and spend the day watching and painting if she wished. These were ways of saying to this girl, "We celebrate the special gifts you have. We are glad you are part of our family."

The special robes are appropriate for birthday celebrations. As the family gathers, the celebrant may be escorted to the table. A toast such as this can be made:

"Let us remember the birth of_____whose presence in our family gives us cause to celebrate."

It may be appropriate then to have one or two persons tell of incidents from the past in which they have been particularly grateful for the presence of this person.

The following liturgy may be used:

Voice 1: Our family is a special circle of people.

Voice 2: Special persons make up our family.

All: We give thanks for our family.

Voice 1: _____brings special happiness to our family.

Voice 2: We are stronger in our fellowship, deeper in our love because of his/her presence.

All: We thank God for_____.
         Let us celebrate birth and life. Let us celebrate a birthday and be sent forth into life in joyful expectation of birthdays to come.

mealtime with friends

This liturgy is planned in lieu of the prayer of blessing when friends come to dinner. If you wish, you can fill small fruit juice glasses for each person at the table. Following the gathering statement, each person is given opportunity to tell about a special memory of a time when members of the two families shared some experience (this can be humorous or serious). The purpose is to help those gathered to recognize the richness of their friendship. When the first person has shared an experience, he or she passes the glass of fruit juice to the next person who then drinks the juice and shares a memory with the group. This continues around the table. Any member of the family may lead the liturgy.

Question: Why are we gathered here?
All: We have come to celebrate common memories and times of being together.
Question: What graces this time and place with such joy and hope and love?
All: The binding power of friendship and the renewing strength of the Holy Spirit.
Request: Let us now symbolize our coming together by sharing common memories and our cups of blessing.

(The above liturgy may be written on small 3" x 5" cards and placed by the juice glass [cup of blessing] of each person at the table.)

166

terrific tuesday

    This time together does not *have* to be on Tuesday, but whatever day you choose as a time of celebration. On the night before announce, "Tomorrow we celebrate a *terrific* day."

    The first definition of the word "terrific" includes such synonyms as "great," "superb," or "magnificent." To encourage a particular outlook on a particular day, family members should be provided with sheets of paper and pencils or crayons on which each person is asked to write or draw something that would make the day truly terrific. These papers are not to be shared until the close of the day. After each person has drawn or written a particular projection, the family may share in this litany.

Voice 1: A whole new day awaits us.

All: This is the day the Lord has made. Rejoice! Be glad in it!

Voice 2: Each of us has the same amount of time in which we live today.

All: This is the day the Lord has made. Rejoice! Be glad in it!

Voice 3: Some of us have busy schedules. Some of us have little that we *must* do.

All: This is the day the Lord has made. Rejoice! Be glad in it!

Voice 4: May we each use the day in a way that makes the time an expression of its own uniqueness.

All: This is the day the Lord has made. Rejoice! Be glad in it!

At the close of the day, come together again and share your pictures or statements. See if the members of the family were able to find a way to make this a "terrific" day for themselves and others.

Listening in Love

If you have not used the song "Love Them Now" since the suggested activity, this may be a good opportunity to sing it again (see pages 78, 79). At this time members of the family will try to determine how well they listen. The first exercise will demonstrate that when persons listen to each other they must hear beyond the words.

Give each member of the family a strip of paper on which is written, "Did you know that?" Then experiment with the sentence by repeating it, emphasizing a different word each time. Young children usually enjoy this game, and it might help the others to sense how tone of voice and facial expressions communicate, too. When the exercise is finished ask someone to read the following poem:

> Heart Learning
> Listening
>   Is giving your whole self to
>   Meanings behind words,
>   Sounds in silences,
>   Sobs in snickering.
> Listening is a lesson
> In learning God's language.
>   Learn it—by heart.
>   —Evelyn Maples

After the poem is shared, ask the individuals to listen to all the sounds in the house. Sometimes it is helpful for a person to close his/her eyes and concentrate on the sounds. If there are teen-agers in your family you may want to play Simon and Garfunkel's "Sounds of Silence" during this time. After about three or four minutes have each person state some of the sounds heard. This can be particularly effective if you plan it for a summer evening outdoors.

There is an excellent skill in human relations called "reflective listening." A person who has learned to listen reflectively is able to mirror back to the speaker that individual's feelings and needs. For instance, if someone comes in and slams down books or packages and announces in a loud voice, "That stupid bus driver makes me furious," chances are this is not the time to call attention to the fact that persons ought not to be called "stupid" or that other people cannot make us furious (we allow ourselves to become furious). The angry individual is not ready to be corrected. The best response to this kind of behavior might be to say, "You sound angry." The person who is infuriated needs to deal with his/her emotions. Reflective listening shows that we hear the feelings as well as the words of others. This also is facilitated when people start giving their thoughts as "I" messages rather than "you" messages. A family can grow into mature relationships when each individual learns to communicate the ideas and feelings that are uniquely his/her own and stops trying to tell another person how he/she feels or thinks. There is an excellent book entitled *Parent Effectiveness Training* which can provide insight into this skill. This method of communication can be shared and discussed with members of the family.

It may be appropriate to have each individual share a time when he/she felt heard by someone else. Then the following may send the family forth to listen more honestly.

Voice 1: Sometimes when someone speaks to me I think I am listening, but I'm really preparing my reply.

All: God, forgive us when we do not listen to each other.

Voice 2: Sometimes when I pray I hurry through. I do not want to hear inside myself that I must be the answer to the prayer. I don't want to listen to God speaking to me in hungry, lonely, loveless people.

All: God, forgive us when we do not listen to each other.

Voice 3: But there are times when I know someone has heard me. When I am angry and no one argues with my anger. When I am happy and no one has to know all the reasons why I act the way I do. Sometimes I feel like saying, "Thank you for hearing me!"

All: Let us listen, let us hear.
Let us listen, let us hear.
Amen.

mother's day, father's day, or children's day

Another occasion for wearing the family celebration robes can be special days—Mother's Day, Father's Day, Children's Day. These are not part of the Christian calendar but have become an established part of modern church observances. It may be that the commercial aspect of these days has provided undesirable emphasis. Perhaps a ritual which can be observed on Mother's Day can be repeated on Father's Day and Children's Day. This particular ritual, rather than romanticizing the role and responsibility of one of the parents or the children, may emphasize the relationship of members of the family to each other. An ideal symbol for this may be lighted candles.

Following a meal together, each member of the family is given a lighted candle. (This should be large enough to burn for some time; a five-inch candle one inch in diameter would be a good size.) The individual candles may be lit from a single one in the center of the table.

Father: We give thanks for this special day. We are remembering not only the gift of_____
                                                    a mother

_____to the family circle
        a father, or children

but also how important each member is to the others.

All: Keep us from exploiting anyone in our family circle.

Mother: We give thanks for this time together. We are grateful for the memories of our shared life. We are deeply thankful for this present moment. We look forward in hope to the future.

All: Keep us loving in the midst of change.

Child: We give thanks for the symbol of the family. This is the place where we find acceptance for ourselves as we are.

All: May grace abound in this family.

Child: We give thanks for special days that remind us of the special nature of each person.

All: May diversity be celebrated.

Child: We give thanks for the forgiveness we have experienced.

Child: We give thanks for the time of play that has enriched our life together.

Child: We give thanks for the work that we sometimes enjoy after it is done.

Child: We give thanks for the sorrow and joy we have known as a family.

All: May we celebrate the peace and tension. Let our life together strengthen the_____
                                                              (mother,
         _____in_____
           father, or children)   (his, her, or their)
         place in our family. Let us symbolize our support for one another.

173

(At this point each person passes the candle to the person on the right.)

We are sent forth with these words:

Child: Bear ye one another's burdens, and so fulfill
         the law of Christ (Gal. 6:2).
All: Lord, make it so.

aNOTHER BIRTHÐAY

This celebration is a time of renewal and remembrance. It is to be held when a member of the family is to be baptized. You may wish to sing the hymn "Morning Has Broken" found in the *First Supplement* to *The Hymnal*. This may provide even richer meaning for the celebration. For those family members who have been baptized, this is an opportunity to remember a special time in their history.

An appropriate symbol for this celebration is a special birthday cake, since this time together gives opportunity to rejoice in the "new birth" in the life of the family. Someone should be prepared to share the covenant statement:

> Having been commissioned of Jesus Christ, I baptize you in the name of the Father, and of the Son, and of the Holy Ghost.

Following the sharing of the covenant statement, members of the family can relate special memories of a baptismal service. This does not have to be the individual's personal experience. There may have been a particular service which became the most meaningful symbol of rebirth. Each person should feel free to share whatever memory is evoked at this time.

After this sharing, the family may want to read together the following or some similar statement:

Voice 1: We are celebrating the making of a covenant.

Voice 2: We are celebrating the gift of God's Spirit.

Voice 3: We are celebrating the "new life" in the community of faith.

All: We are celebrating baptism!

Someone who has experienced baptism: I remember the physical act of going into the water.

Someone who has experienced confirmation: I remember the physical act of having hands laid on my head.

All: Let us celebrate promises made.
          Let us celebrate God's kept promise to us.
          Let us celebrate the gift of the Holy Spirit.

Voice 1: We have come to sense a call to be immersed in human needs.

Voice 2: We have come to see the power of the Holy Spirit that makes us uncomfortable when others suffer.

Voice 3: We have come to feel responsibility for the needs of others.

All: We have come to celebrate baptism.
          Send us forth to be your people—reborn, made new.
          Make it so, Lord,
          Make it so! Amen.

After the reading together, the newly baptized

member may cut the cake. Glasses of punch can be served at which time the members of the family may wish to toast the newly baptized person.

sent forth in love

There are times when one member of the family leaves the home for a while. When this happens the departing person can be strengthened by some symbolic act or ritual which says, "You are supported in your new situation by persons who love you and celebrate your new opportunity." Candles may be used in a meaningful way for this celebration. It may be appropriate to purchase a large candle to be lit when the person returns home from time to time. And a candle sent with the person departing can serve as a reminder of the support of the family.

Each member is given an unlit candle and seated at a table on which one large candle is placed. The glow from this should be the only light in the room.

The person who is being sent forth is the first to light a candle. He/she may express feelings experienced as the time for leaving draws near. The others may want to respond by saying:

> "We send you forth.
> We encircle you with love and free you
> with trust.
> We send you forth."

Following this, the individual who has spoken lights his/her candle. Then each member of the family offers a statement of support, such as "I hope the coming months will be the best time you have ever known," or "I wish you success in your new opportunity," or "May you know that you are loved while you are gone." Each of these statements will be followed by

> "We send you forth.
> We encircle you with love and free you
> with trust.
> We send you forth."

After each statement, the speaker lights a candle until each one is lit. The family members then stand and hold their candles while one member of the family offers a sending-forth prayer.

called into community

This activity is designed to be used during the observance of Trinity. It may be most appropriate in the fall, particularly if school has just begun and some members of the family are coping with new relationships.

Paul's letter to the saints at Philippi may be of help at a time when new experiences seem threatening.

The members of the family may be called together by the reading of the following scripture:

Does your life in Christ make you strong?
Does his love comfort you? Do you have fellowship with his Spirit?
Do you feel kindness and compassion for one another?
—Philippians 2:1.

The song, "The Church Within Us," found in the *First Supplement to The Hymnal* No. S-4, may be introduced here. The family members may want to sing this together. Some of the stanzas introduce ideas that may stimulate discussion. Time for this should be allowed. Then each person shares an experience of the day in which he/she felt there was an opportunity to "be the church." For young children, this concept may be described as "a chance to make someone feel loved and important."

Then the following may be shared:

Voice 1: God, you send us out from the family each
day.
Voice 2: Send us out to comfort.
Voice 3: Send us out to show kindness.
Voice 4: Send us out to offer compassion.
All: Make us strong in your Spirit.
Make us strong in your love.
Help us to share the church within us,
O Lord.
The family is sent forth by again singing "The
Church Within Us."

the family covenants together

A covenant is an agreement between two persons or
a group of people. It is a promise that they will support
and help each other. A husband and wife are living in
a covenant relationship made when they were
married. The members of the family may want to
explore the possibility of writing a covenant together
which can be referred to and evaluated as they struggle
to move into areas of concern in the community and to
support each other in individual expressions of mission.
They may want to gather at the table and share the
following information.

In the Old Testament (Numbers 18:19, II Chronicles
13:5, and Ezra 4:14) reference is made to a "salt
covenant" since eating salt with someone means to be
bound to him in loyalty. Salt was seen not only as a

preservative but a symbol of fellowship. This carries over to an expression used in modern-day Arab communities by persons who speak of "salt between us" and to Western cultures where the phrase "to share a man's salt" describes a meaningful meal with a friend. After this is explained to the family, one person takes the saltshaker and shakes a small amount of salt into the palm of the hand of the person to his/her right. As this is done the statement, "I covenant to support you as a friend," may be made. This continues around the table.

When the salt ritual has been concluded, the family may want to work together to create a statement of mutual covenant. This can be specific so that sometime during the week it may be evaluated. For instance a covenant may read: "This week we, the_____

family, covenant to be more caring for one another and others. We promise to listen to each other and try to express our feelings honestly."

When the covenant is completed, each person should sign it. It is most important that the creation of the covenant be so structured that even the youngest has some opportunity for expression. (In one family with a small infant the handprint of the baby was placed on the written statement of covenant.) This written statement can be lengthy or simple. It should be referred to at later times. The family may want to write a covenant periodically.

The sharing of salt is a symbolic act. Appropriate for use with it is a statement attributed to Jesus (Matthew 5:13 and Mark 9:50): "You are like salt for all mankind. . . . Salt is good. But if it loses its saltness, how can you make it salty again? Have salt in yourselves, and be at peace with one another" (TEV).

Voice 1: We have tasted the salt.
All: We have covenanted together.
Voice 2: Our lives are flavored by God's love, just as the salt flavors our food.
All: We have covenanted together.
Voice 3: God calls us to live in peace with one another and to share his love.
All: We have covenanted together. Amen.

opportunities for worship

There may be times in the family's life when the setting lends itself so ideally to worship that the spontaneous, natural response to the situation *is* worship. There may be opportunities which are overlooked. Here are some possibilities. One family discovered the *Chronicles of Narnia* by C. S. Lewis when the mother read the books aloud as they traveled across their native land. She found herself reading by flashlight one night when the trip did not include an overnight stop. That was a special, memorable trip for the entire family. Another family reads Volume One of this series, *The Lion, the Witch and the Wardrobe*, each year at Christmastime. Reading aloud can be delightful and can lead the family into a worship activity.

Certain occasions create opportunities for worship. The death of a pet, the birth or adoption of a baby, an engagement, a first job, a wedding, the beginning of a season, a spring rainfall, a baby's first step, a specific assignment finished are all special times. Some of these experiences can provide a setting in which the mighty acts of God are affirmed.

Learning new songs can be a joyful experience for the family. Young children like to sing. Learning to appreciate the musical tastes of each person can enrich

182

relationships in the home. This, too, can provide a setting in which worship may occur.

Perhaps sensitivity to each other and to the "greater than any of us" is the key to building a climate in which worship can take place. Dietrich Bonhoeffer is known in many circles as an outstanding German theologian-martyr who was killed by the Nazis in 1945. He was a pastor and worked in the underground church during the time of Hitler's rise to power. He came from a Christian family who loved and nurtured him through his struggles and decisions. When he was imprisoned, he found opportunities to search for ways to understand what it meant to belong to God. He found himself strengthened by the love and support of his family. He faced the prison trials as a person whose life-style had been established in his home. Much that

is known about him is found in letters written to members of his family. His writings speak to families today, and what he says reflects his own relationship with his family and his convictions regarding the value of Christian worship. While his experience may not be the experience of every person, it offers insight and conviction:

Common life under the Word begins with common worship at the beginning of the day. The family community gathers for praise and thanks, reading of the Scriptures and prayer. The deep stillness of morning is broken first by the prayer and song of the fellowship. After the silence of night and early morning, hymns and the Word of God are more easily grasped. . . . For Christians the beginning of the day should not be burdened and oppressed with besetting concerns for the day's work. At the threshold of the new day stands the Lord who made it. . . . Therefore, at the beginning of the day let all distraction and empty talk be silenced and let the first thought and the first word belong to Him to whom our whole life belongs.

Dietrich Bonhoeffer — *Life Together.*

Worship in the early morning may not be possible for all of us but Bonhoeffer's testimony can be ours: We belong to God who sustains us through all the days of our lives. When as a family we can share in this awareness, worship occurs.

BIBLIOGRAPHY

Balloons Belong in Church—family worship resources for all ages
   prepared by Moravian Church in America, paperback.
Bell, Martin. *The Way of the Wolf.* New York: Seabury Press,
   1971.
Benson, Dennis. *Electric Liturgy.* Richmond: John Knox Press,
   1972.
_____. *Celebrations: 4 Cassette Tapes.* Nashville: Abingdon,
   1973.
Brenner, Scott Francis. *Ways of Worship for New Forms of
   Mission.* New York: Friendship, 1968.
Carroll, James. *Wonder and Worship.* Paramus: Paulist Press,
   1973.
Davies, J. G. *Worship and Mission.* New York: Association Press,
   1967.
Davies, J. G. (ed.) *A Dictionary of Liturgy and Worship.* New
   York: Macmillan, 1972.
Gibson, George M. *The Story of the Christian Year.* Nashville:
   Abingdon, 1945.
Hoon, Paul Waitman. *The Integrity of Worship.* Nashville:
   Abingdon, 1971.
Horn, Henry E. *Worship in Crisis.* Philadelphia: Fortress Press,
   1972.
Hovda, Robert W., and Huck, Gabe. *There's No Place Like
   People: Planning Small Group Liturgies.* Chicago: Argus
   Communications, 1971.
Jansen, John Frederick. *Let Us Worship God.* Richmond: CLC
   Press, 1966.
Keen, Sam. *To a Dancing God.* New York: Harper and Row,
   1970.
Kreml, Anne Lee. Family Actualization Scale included in an
   unpublished thesis *Understanding Conflict in the Normal*

Family: An Educational Model for Family Actualization.
Chicago Theological Seminary, June, 1970.

Lundin, Jack. *Celebrations for Special Days and Occasions.* New York: Harper & Row.

Mead, Loren B. *New Hope for Congregations.* New York: Seabury Press, 1972.

O'Conner, Elizabeth. *Eighth Day of Creation.* Waco: Word Books, 1972.

Oden, Thomas. *The Rhythm of the Celebrating Community,* paper.

Paulus, Trina, *Hope for the Flowers.* Paramus: Paulist Press, 1973.

Reid, Clyde. *Celebrate the Temporary.* New York: Harper & Row, 1972.

Rochelle, Jay C. *Create and Celebrate.* Philadelphia: Fortress Press, 1971.

Sloyan, Virginia, and Huck, Gabe (eds.). *Children's Liturgies.* Washington: The Liturgical Conference, 1970.

Snyder, Ross. *Contemporary Celebration.* Nashville: Abingdon Press, 1971.

_____ *Inscape.* Nashville: Abingdon Press, 1968.

Underhill, Evelyn. *Worship.* New York: Harper & Row, 1957.

Weiser, Francis X. *Handbook of Christian Feasts and Customs.* New York: Harcourt Brace & Co., 1952.

White, James F. *New Forms of Worship.* Nashville: Abingdon Press, 1971.

Zdenek, Marilee, and Marge Champion. *Catch the New Wind.* Waco: Word Books, 1973.

186